FAITH
OF OUR
FATHERS

VOLUME FIVE

A New Christian Nation

Louis Weeks

A Consortium Book

Copyright © 1977 by McGrath Publishing Company
Manufactured in the United States of America

Library of Congress Card Catalog Number: 77-9553
ISBN: 0-8434-0624-0
ISBN: 0-8434-0637-2 paper

To Mary Weeks
Doretta Mang
Sidney Mang
with thanks

Table of Contents

1

Toward A Christian America

The prospect of the new nation becoming indeed a Christian one was a compelling thought to church folk in 1790. The United States offered proof positive that change could be accomplished. The "Laws of Nature and Nature's God," as Thomas Jefferson so neatly articulated the feelings of patriots, simply required a measure of Christian commitment from the people. To many evangelical Christians (certainly not to Jefferson himself) these laws were more than regular evidence of divine providence; the very existence of America provided convincing argument of God's miraculous grace, His special affection for the New World.

Very little in the new country led the unbelieving and the marginally committed to a similar conclusion concerning the state of American religion. They perceived a minimum of piety in the people, crassness, even chaos, in the structures, and human initiative in abundance. The nation's few Catholics and fewer Jews, not to mention the national majority of irreligious persons, still recognized the United States as "Protestant," however. While church strength appeared minute—perhaps ten percent of the population—a pervasive sense of "righteous empire" infected almost every one of the white Americans at the time.

To America's West lay vast amounts of free land, a frontier already summoning the adventurous pioneers and the malcontents of the seaboard states, and likewise offering temporary haven to displaced indigenous populations and still a permanent home for hundreds of "native" American tribes. Yet as cartographers, religious, pioneers, slaves, settlers, immigrants, European diplomats, and other people viewed the nation, it was for better or worse, "Protestant."

During the decades under present scrutiny, 1790-1865, the nation consolidated its holdings (both spiritual and physical) while at the same time multiplying itself in phenomenal growth. Historians would agree, at least during the first portion of the twentieth century, that "free space" to the frontier of America was a primary (if not the determinative) element in establishing a national mind and an American spirit. Thus during the decades under consideration, the "Old Northwest" and Missouri lands, the Cumberland Gap, post roads, Erie Canal, and myriad other national landmarks given and created became symbols of a manifest American destiny, a Providential guiding of the people.

The religion of the new nation can be recounted in a variety of ways: politically, structurally, in popular fashion, even in terms of psychohistory. But the recognized and organized communions of the United States—primarily Protestant, but also Catholic and Jewish—offer perhaps the crispest insight into the role of religion in the formation of the new country.

The Aftermath of the Revolution

The newly formed United States of America had represented itself as a nation, even under its Articles of Confederation. But only as the Federalists gained in strength through America's first constitutional election of 1789 did the country appear securely one. George Washington, inaugurated on April 30, wore a sword along with his brown clothes and white stockings. And he took the oath of office by placing his hand on a Bible. As a matter of fact, before Samuel Otis, the Secretary of the Senate, could lift the book, Washington bowed to kiss it. Both sword and scripture were implements for the building of the new nation. Washington spoke of the "providential agency" which had instigated the great revolution now being culminated by electoral processes, and the new President gave credit for all things to "the Great Author of every public and private good."

With the ratification of the Bill of Rights in 1791, a "federalism" was insured for decades to follow. For a dozen years the Federalist Party itself would control the Presidency. Then through a presidential succession of Democratic-Republican, Democrat, Whig, Democrat, Whig, Democrat the process moved, until with Republican Abraham Lincoln elected in 1860, the South would withdraw from the precarious Union.

The story of those political parties and institutions, and of the people leading them, constitutes one history of the period. It is a "religious" history, for the very mythology which arose to surround these people and places has yielded a measure of sanctity and transcendental significance for them. Moreover, a commonly accepted "religion," civil in its substance, came to occupy the American mind and heart before the time of the Civil War. The Revolutionary War came to be viewed as a new Exodus, a miraculous happening designed to deliver the American people into a Promised Land. Sacred shrines arose — the Capitol, a White House, and various monuments. Respect for Washington as a person turned quickly to awe, and he was remembered as a reincarnation of Moses. Other guiding lights achieved the status of demi-gods in the eyes of many Americans. And an orthodoxy of public belief evolved—sectionally-oriented but doctrinally discernable. "Progress," "destiny," "mission," and "rights" became some of the *loci* of popular faith. And the story is discernable alongside others as one historical sequence in the aftermath of the Revolution.

Likewise the United States in the wake of the war which grasped for independence began to exercise the martial arts. The story of the nation's wars, especially the indecisiveness of the War of 1812, the militancy of the Monroe Doctrine, its attendant skirmishes, the ambiguity of the Mexican War, the tragedy of the Indian Wars of attrition, and the catastrophic Civil War, is yet another perspective from which to learn of the American experience.

Here too the story is a religious one, whether the recounting consists in the reciting of sequential "crusades" by heroes against various external (heathen?) forces, of the anti-war pacifist groups, or of both. Military *foci* include the scriptural, mythical, and ethical underpinnings of each range of combatants. And quickly the military history as a religious story in the United States becomes a very complicated affair.

To take but one, and in many respects "simple," example of this pattern, consider the religious dimensions of the struggle between "settlers" and "indigenous populations" during these times. On the one hand, some whites felt divinely compelled by God to pursue their special duty and to occupy for development the lands recklessly squandered by the heathen "Indians." To most of these persons, "savages" had few rights if any at all. Like the Afro-American people imported into slavery, these "colored" people were seen as inferior beings, "human wards" of the mature whites.

By the same token, the religion of many tribes of "indigenous peoples" included mythic stories of having wandered into their present lands as well, of their occupation of "promised" territories. Subsequently, anthropologists have discerned that in fact the peoples termed "Indians" did come from portions of Asia and had themselves wrested lands from other tribes there from even earlier migrations. But Indian tribes also told in their religion of people who, migrating Westward, had dropped from the face of the earth. They held the land in which they lived both because of divine bestowal and also because of fear of obliteration should they return Westward. Thus it proved quite natural for them to resist all types of incursion which sought to send them packing, to dispossess them.

This history, as a religious aftermath of the American

Revolution, is extremely difficult to relate. In fact since many of the Indian sources are not available, telling it truly is downright impossible. But records indicate some portions of the contests. Cherokees, for instance, were supported in Congress by some Southerners, not just by Representatives and Senators from the Northeast. But it was Theodore Frelinghuysen of New Jersey who spoke perhaps most eloquently of God's care for the rights of Indians:

> God, in his providence, planted these tribes on this western continent, so far as we know, before Great Britain herself had a political existence.... They have a place in human sympathy, and are just as entitled to a share in the common bounties of a benignant Providence.... We have crowded the tribes upon a few miserable acres of our southern frontier; it is all that is left to them of their once boundless forest.... I ask, who is the injured, and who is the aggressor?

Despite the cogent objections of Frelinghuysen and others, Congress did pass the Indian Removal Act of 1830, just another needed piece of legislation to some people but a seeming act of genocide to several tribes of Indians. Soldiers forced the southeastern tribes westward. Numerous incidents of cruelty and hostility accompanied the implementation of this violent law, and they were matched by many such actions in the Western territories also.

Not only is it a difficult project to recount this pattern of interaction with its religious implications, the lack of documents makes such a story downright impossible to relate. Only the Cherokee tribe offered a decipherable, written language; and the sources for even that point of view are for the most part lost. Another factor was the incredible diversity of the Indian peoples. Tribes varied as much as, if not more than, the incoming settlers. People in more than 200 linguistic groups, and a greater number of tribal groups, inhabited America north of Mexico in 1790. Lewis and Clark recorded their reactions to multiferous tongues, attitudes, levels of belligerency, and religious beliefs as they explored the frontier. In New England severe impingement already threatened the Pennacooks, Nipmucs, Massachusetts, Narragansetts, Mohegans, and other groups. During the decades under present consideration encroachments either destroyed or seriously changed the Mohawk, Oneida, Onondaga, Cayuga, Senaca, and Tuscarora tribes, the Six Nations of the League of the Iroquois; the Sawk, Fox, Potawatomis, Menomines, and other Algonquin peoples of the Great Lakes; the Kaskaskias, Peorias, and other members of the Illinois Confederacy; the independent Shawnee who hunted in Appalachia, the Gulf tribes of Creeks, Seminole, Chickasaw, and Tunicas, not to mention the cultured Cherokee already discussed.

Here then are two ways of recounting religious "growth" in the new nation; but members of other ways of telling the story beg for attention—how the religious life of Americans underwent gradual democratization during these decades, a process which went hand in hand with political reconstitution; how American religious discipline declined; or how the core of American religious cults and symbols moved from the country to the city. All these themes will be mentioned in the present interpretation of the times, but primarily this history will recount the movement of dissenting religious peoples into the mainstream of American religion.

Continuing and emergent denominations and movements provided a socially coherent underpinning for incipient American society. In the East dissent seems at times to have been the more thoroughgoing, the more radical. In the West dissenters appear to have achieved more stability and a greater portion of their objectives. In the South, dissent from national patterns of behavior in matters religious was more focused on the institutions of and surrounding slavery. In the North, perhaps greater diffusion in issues yielded more cultural diversity. But in the aftermath of the American Revolutionary War, American religion grew to become enormously important as a portion of national life. Group by group, movement by movement, this story moves to encompass American class, economic, cultural, educational, family, and political life. It remains indeed astounding how much actual change occurred between 1790 and 1865, and the change meant growth in the numbers of churches as well as in their strength.

The Strength of the Churches

Already by the time William Cobbett, the English reformer and radical, visited New York in 1818, American churches had gained considerable strength. "Here are plenty of churches," he reported: "three Episcopal (English) Churches; three Presbyterian Churches; three Lutheran Churches; one or two Quaker Meetinghouses; and two Methodist places; all within *six miles* of the spot where I am sitting." Cobbett pointed out further that all were handsome and in "neatest order," and he concluded that as a direct result the American people in that city "are the most orderly, sensible, and least criminal people in the whole world."

Churches in New York, and those throughout the country, had grown enormously in the years since the War. By all accounts at the close of the Revolution a low ebb in religious sentiments existed, a point of indifference never again paralleled. So long as Protestant antipathy focused on the Anglican Establishment, the prospect of an American bishop, and the new church power in the colonies, the vitality of the churches appeared intact. Before and even during the Revolution the finding and isolating of Anglican "scapegoats" allowed a tacit pact between Reformed and other dissenting Christians. Robert Carter, III, a wealthy Virginia planter and vestryman without fervor in the nearby Cople Parish, became a Baptist in 1777 in part because Philip Fithian, a Presbyterian, led him to read sermons by the nondenominational George Whitefield. As a Baptist, Carter entertained not only John Leland, missionary of that communion, but Tirah Tamplin, the Presbyterian, as well. Fi-

nally Carter moved to Baltimore and became a Swedenbor-
gian before his death in 1804.

The alliance was solidified by the Quebec Act of 1774,
which granted rights to French-speaking Catholics. Free
Church members in the colonies viewed this action of Parlia-
ment to be almost as heinous as the Coercive Acts of the same
year which closed the port of Boston and provided impunity,
forced hospitality, and new legal powers to soldiers of the
crown. Was the Anglican nod toward papal authority an
augur of things to come, a portent of further incursions by
the crown on freedom of worship? Was the Church of England
about to heal its breach with the Church of Rome?

During the struggle itself, religious questions remained
crucial ones. Even though a number of clergy had joined laypeople in forsaking the sanctuary for the battlefield, the
churches seemed to remain vibrant institutions. After the
War, however, religious observance came to "hard times."
Estimates vary, but probably at the most about ten percent of
the white population and fewer of the blacks, free or slave,
were church folk at the time of the first American census in
1790.

Figures which are both accurate and illuminating for that
early date are difficult to obtain. The census itself was a rudimentary affair, determining exclusively the various populations for the purpose of governmental representation. Census
takers determined America's aggregate white population in
that year to be 3,172,464, counting all the whites in the
thirteen original states and four others joined or joining. The
free black population, 59,466; and slaves, numbering
697,897. Thus church strength, as a small portion of the
white and even smaller, of the black, proved minute indeed.

The "Second Great Awakening," the revival movement of
the period which began in the late 1780's at Hampden-Syd-
ney College in Prince Edward County, Virginia, and cropped
up subsequently in many New England towns as well as in
the South, added large numbers of believers to the various
communions in the Protestant spectrum. By one reliable ac-

count, the number of Methodists in the U.S. doubled in a matter of but eight years—between 1796 and 1804 their numbers increased from 56,664 to 115,411. Likewise Presbyterians, Baptists, and Congregational churches grew considerably.

The Camp-Meeting, a refinement on the revival phenomenon involving marathon worship services and a smorgasbord of different preaching styles, began in the early 1800's to multiply church membership again for the communions so inclined to employ it. But the immigration of new Americans with pious heritages also affected growth in a positive fashion. A third factor helped too—the establishment of permanent congregations of all varieties in the various urban areas. Doubtless, other important reasons can be given for church growth—the greater mobility of ministers with the elongation of far-reaching "post-roads" and the creation of canal systems; the establishment of railroads throughout much of the nation, the new theological currents for and against reform, Biblical authority and criticism, the educational movements, and attitudes of competition and ecumenism. Whatever the myriad, sometimes conflicting factors, growth occurred.

Baptists gains were perhaps the most miraculous and the most impressive, because their churches in the West frequently disparaged any missionary involvement in church development and sometimes Baptists opposed all revival techniques. Despite (or perhaps because of) these hinderances, adherents of the communions of Baptists increased at least ten-fold between the turn of the century and the beginning of the Civil War. From about 100,000 communicants in 1800, the Baptists grew to claim at least a million members in 1860. Since they counted only adult members, their numbers would probably swell even more in comparison with churches practicing infant baptism.

Methodist growth, more understandable in light of their circuit-riding clergy and coordinated lay leadership, their good organiztion and personable bishopric, was even greater than that of the Baptists. About 70,000 members in 1800 became close to two million by the opening of the War.

Reformed churches grew also, though less dramatically. The 100,000 or so Congregationalists and Presbyterians at the beginning of the century became about seven times that many by 1860; and German and Dutch Reformed communions numbered another 150,000 at least. Unitarian and Universalist Churches had grown during these years, too, as an offshoot of the liberal wing of the Reformed bodies.

Lutheran growth, considerable also, came more from new immigrations than from conversions. The same kind of growth may have accounted for the rapid increase in Episcopalian membership. Quaker growth, less telling that that of most other communions, probably was stymied by the Hicksite controversy and split.

Catholic believers began flocking to America during the period after 1830, as Irish immigrants joined the English, German, and even French migratory streams already in progress. Portions of families told relatives of their opportunities, and perchance even helped them in moving.

Jewish population increased also, and according to the data on church accommodations in 1850, synagogues showed space for 19,588 at worship.

That table concerning church accommodation yields interesting information about the Christian communions as well. Methodists, for example, provided worship facilities for 4,354,101. Their greatest number of available places was in Ohio (543,490) and the least, in California (1,600). Generally the Methodist "spread" proves the most even of all the churches too. Baptists, second numerically with pews for 3,248,580 in the 32 states and four territories of the day, exhibited greatest strength in New York (335,374), Georgia (321,668), Kentucky (288,455), and Virginia (247,589). Presbyterians, third with about 2,000,000 seats, focused their efforts also in New York, but Pennsylvania and Ohio ranked second and third for them. Following in order of their numbers are Congregational (801,835), Catholic (675,721), Episcopal (644,598), Lutheran (535,180), Christian (304,630), Friends (287,073), Universalist (214,965), Union (201,864), Dutch Reformed (180,636), German Reformed (159,338), and Unitarian (136,417). Moravian and "Free" (church-space that was shared by differing denominations, usually on the frontier) equalled about 100,000 each. A montage of "Minor Sects," groups already proliferating in members and theological diversity, in 1850 claimed about 150,000 places for worship. The census takers found Albright, Associate Reformed, Covenanters, Campellites, Church of Brotherly Love, Church of God, Disciples, Dissenters, Emanuels, Evangelicals, Winebrenians, Whitfield, and about ten others which they named before they resigned with an "etc."

A note at the bottom of the table indicated that the Catholics "have no doubt more actual worshippers than they can accommodate at one sitting in their churches. Catholics represented a distinct minority, however, in that respect. For the 23,191,873 inhabitants of the U.S. in 1850 (only 19,553,068 of whom were white) had 14,270,139 seats in churches, roughly two seats for each 3 people. The U.S. had already "outchurched" England, where in 1850 there were accommodations for only 57% of the population in their churches.

American movements toward greater prosperity and toward urbanized living also proved significant during the time frame under scrutiny. Per capita wealth increased from $191 in 1790 to $590 per person in 1860. And in 1790, only six cities possessed populations of more than 8,000—Philadelphia, Boston, New York, Baltimore, Salem, and Charleston. Each of these urban areas served as a major seaport. By 1860 commercial and industrial centers dotted the inland landscape as well as encircling the eastern half of the continental United States at its shoreline.

The chief exception to the general rules of American urbanization and increased prosperity was that of black America, which though also becoming predominantly Christian remained largely slave and rural. They had no rights in sight, as slaves, and few, as freed or free people. Thus to speak of "church strength" among black America becomes quite a different narrative. To be sure denominations did develop during these years, and they counted statistics as did the predominantly white communions. But for the most part black churches found increased strength which remained totally unreported, loosely organized (sometimes out of necessity), and otherworldly in orientation.

As for the predominantly white churches, both the mainstream communions and the emerging sects viewed the idea of progress as a "title read clear," a ready possession, a presupposition taken for granted. The kingdom of God moved inexorably toward their own theological positions. Few people in the 1850's could foresee any shattering of this unmitigated church advance. Only liberal fringes of the Protestant communions supported labor organizations, abolition of slavery, women's rights, or others of the now obvious starting points for social amelioration. But they viewed themselves, in the words of Horace Bushnell, a first-rate theologian of the times, as "the grand experiment of Protestantism.... set to show.... the moral capabilities and the beneficent fruits of Christianity and the Protestant Faith."

The Challenge of the Frontier

The Frenchman and uneasy liberal Alexis de Tocqueville waxed eloquent on the subject of America's frontier. "Millions of men are marching at once toward the same horizon," he reported grandiloquently. "Their language, their religion, their manners differ, their object is the same. The gifts of fortune are promised in the West, and to the West they bend their course." The frontier, of which de Tocqueville spoke so glowingly was that of the Ohio and Mississippi River valleys. And the frontier in turn affected the manners and morals of all Americans, according to him. He found that those persons on the frontier exhibited the most striking opposites in behavior. Ohioans, de Tocqueville discovered to have focused upon "temporal prosperity as the chief aim" of life. Across the river, however, he discovered the slave-owning people of Kentucky to be quite different. "The Kentuckian scorns not only labor, but all undertakings that labor promotes," de Tocqueville declared. "As he lives in idle independence, his tastes are those of an idle man."

This was the West of the 1830's, at least as one observant person described it, a blend of common experience of the ever progressing frontier and the juxtaposition of opposites. Even granting the Frenchman's hyperbole, truth lay in his assertions. Strange, though, that de Tocqueville identified the Kentuckian with an idle slave-owner! There, as indeed throughout the West, a thoroughly mixed population dwelled together. Catholics had come early to this territory, for example, as members of the Coomes family settled first in Harrodsburg in 1775 and later in Bardstown. The Coomes gave some land to the Church, and priests Stephen T. Badin and Michael Barriere arrived there in 1793. Badin, who remained when Barriere returned to more comfortable quarters, continued to minister to a growing number of Catholics until permanent assistance arrived in 1805. It was only a matter of three years before Bardstown became the suffragen bishopric for all the frontier not including the Louisiana Territory.

Kentucky, with all its Catholic population, drew one-fourth of all Virginia Baptists and a great number of like minded people from other states between 1791 and 1810. It gave free-space to them also, and to their cousins settling simultaneously in Tennessee. Frontier Baptists frequently made common cause with Methodists, Presbyterians, and other evangelicals. The camp-meetings seem to have had space for all, at least early in the movement before denominations themselves began to exploit the phenomenon. To Father Badin the revivals, with quickie conversions and even speedier celebrations of baptism, represented a detestable cheapening of the religious experience. "They Baptize incessantly men who know not even the intent of baptism far from knowing the discriminating doctrines of the church...." he lamented. Of course, many middle-class Presbyterians took a dim view of the goings-on also, despite Father Badin's accusation that "the Presbyterians have thought proper to imitate the tricks" of the Baptists. But the point of the matter remains that all found a supportive environment when surrounded by some like-minded persons even when dissenting from some not-so-like-minded.

Although he did not recount the experience of Badin and the Baptists, the historian Frederick Jackson Turner set this direction for interpreting the American experience when he read "The Significance of the Frontier in American History" at an 1893 meeting of the American Historical Association. "The existence of an area of free land, its continuous recession, and the advance of American settlement westward, explain American development," Turner explained. What was uniquely American—the fluidity of life, a new sense of opportunity, an almost primitive simplicity, and other characteristics—resulted from the continuous incorporation of new frontiers into the mainstream of national life.

"When the first census was taken in 1790," Turner pointed out, "the continuous settled area was bounded by a line which ran near the coast of Maine, and included New England, except a portion of Vermont and New Hampshire, New York along the Hudson and up the Mohawk about Schenectady, eastern and southern Pennsylvania, Virginia well across the Shenandoah Valley, and the Carolinas and eastern Georgia." Beyond this line lay "the West," another self-conscious section in development.

By the time of the 1820 census, the frontier lay "along the Great Lakes... and beyond the Mississippi." But by the middle of the century, according to Turner, "the line indicated by the present [1893] eastern boundary of Indian Territory, Nebraska and Kansas marked "a frontier. Frontier conditions existed in Minnesota and Wisconsin, but the "distinctive frontier of the period" was in California. Turner quoted a long passage from Peck's *New Guide to the West*, 1832, (here condensed) which told of the frontier cycle:

> Generally, in all the western settlements, three classes, like the waves of the ocean, have rolled one after the other. First comes the pioneer.... The next class of emigrants purchase the lands...and exhibit the picture and forms of plain, frugal, civilized life. Another wave rolls on. The men of capital and enterprise come. The settler is ready to sell out.... Thus wave after wave is rolling westward; the real Eldorado is still farther on....

The Turner thesis has been subjected to critical scrutiny ever since its formulation, but portions of that hypothesis remain as a cogent interpretation for discerning the period under present examination. One good question, put by a number of scholars, asks, "The frontier of what?" They argue that constantly the American frontier consisted in the repetition of patterns of behavior to which European peoples had been accustomed in their lands of origin. The Rappites, for instance, built houses like the ones they had left and they coaxed the land to produce crops they already knew how to cook. They flourished in New Harmony, on the Indiana frontier; and other settlers did not have to be so communally oriented in order to "bring" European ideas and institutions with them. Whole countries grew from timberlands or river valleys into prosperous communities of German, Scotch-Irish, or Scandinavian folk within the space of one generation. The discipline and social institutions quickly invoked were those brought from the various homelands from which they came.

But the need for discipline was perhaps greatest on the frontiers. The sheer logistics of transporting grain, for instance, simply begged for its reduction into potable spirits. The horse carrying four bushels of grain could carry the liquid equivalent of six times that much. And to compound the economics of the situation, the price of liquor remained comparatively stable in contrast with mercuric changes in the price of corn. No wonder more than half the cases of church discipline apparently included accusations of drunkenness and intemperance. No wonder a temperance movement grew to respond to the increase in American consumption of alcoholic beverages, a rise in the drinking of hard liquor from about 2½ gallons per person per year in 1792 to over 7½ in 1823. Societal discipline and reform became a natural cultural result of the frontier phenomenon, whatever other causes might have also affected it in addition.

Another serious limitation of the Turner thesis was its assumption that the frontier enabled unparalleled upward mobility among American whites. Again, Turner quoted Peck to assert "A portion of the first two classes remain stationary amidst the general movement, improve their habits and condition, and rise in the scale of society." Turner concluded that this claim by Peck was a true one, that "the most important effect of the frontier has been in the promotion of democracy here and in Europe." By way of contrast, more recent scholars have discerned that the middle class immigrants were the ones who settled the frontier during the nineteenth century. They were the people possessing the $1000 or more (in 1860) necessary for purchasing equipment and passage, land and food until the first good harvest. The poor immigrant was the more likely person to move to a city in the new country, and by at least one account twenty children from the farms of America migrated to urban areas for every malcontent that left the city for the frontier farm.

Be that as it may, the religious institutions which increased dramatically in strength during this period evidenced a constant interaction between the frontier and the stable yet growing urban centers. Lyman Beecher, "the Big Gun of Calvinism," who lived from 1775 until 1863, inculcated personally this organic symbiosis of the East and the frontier.

Born in New Haven, in the blacksmith family of David and Esther Beecher, he attended Yale under Timothy Dwight. Ordained in 1799 as a Presbyterian (he also married that year, to Roxana Foote), Lyman ministered first in East Hampton and then in Litchfield. He sought in both places, and with mixed results, to foster a "continuous revival" among the people. Revivalism, a movement with its greatest strength in the frontier-like section of the country, had already become accepted by eastern church-folk in many congregations. When Beecher received his call to come to Boston, the intellectual "hub of the universe" as citizens of that community modestly termed their city, Beecher went preaching fiercely in favor of redemption and Christian living, against the rum houses and the Catholic immigrants. A series of his nativist sermons against the power of the pope, the hordes of new Catholics, and the monastic ideal evidently led in part to the burning of an Ursuline Convent in nearby Charlestown. The tolerance of Kentucky nativists toward Catholic neighbors found scant parallel in the centers of culture.

Beecher surprised his supporters and critics alike when, after six and one half years in Boston he accepted the call from the newly-formed Lane Theological Seminary in Cincinnati and moved westward in 1832 with his family to become its first president. Always preaching, whatever the occasion, he seized the moment for an eloquent "Plea for the West," a call upon all Americans to support the western thrust of the nation:

> It is equally plain that the religious and political destiny of our nation is to be decided in the West. . . . A nation is being 'born in a day'. . . . But what will become of the West if her prosperity rushes up to such a majesty of power, while those great institutions linger which are necessary to form the mind and the conscience and the heart of that vast world.

Beecher argued forcefully that not only his own, but indeed every American's future was inextricably bound to the West. "Let no man of the East quiet himself and dream of liberty," he declared; the destiny of the West was "our destiny." Beecher himself stood trial for heresy, his accuser J.L. Wilson arguing that the revivalist gave little credence to the Westminster Standards. Typical of many Western matters, however, the case remained unresolved in essence and contributed finally to a Presbyterian split in 1837, 1838 along doctrinal, ethical, and sectional lines. Beecher resigned in 1850 and moved back East to Brooklyn, where his son Henry Ward had been preaching for some time.

Granting that Beecher was a leader, not an ordinary citizen and layperson in the church, and granting that the focal point of his Western activity was scarcely a rude frontier at the time of his arrival, it remains important that his living dialogue between America East and America West was representative of the interaction of the people of his day. Each group and movement lived in a dialectic of seaboard and frontier; and a fascinating synthesis resulted.

2

Established American Religious Communions

As pensioners already on their ecclesiastical ancestors, the churchpeople of the times looked back to the Great Awakening as a golden time in the religious history of America. More than that, many took the revival model as a viable one for the future. In the words of Mark Hopkins, President of Williams, a "triumph of Christianity" would bring about the "perfection of society." Jewish people certainly modified such a contention to include themselves, and many denominations would also substitute their own brand of Christianity for the general term. But that a societal burden lay on the religious bodies for perfecting the nation remained seldom a subject of contention.

The Methodists, consonant with their Arminian theology, brought a concerned and concerted voice throughout locations and circuits alike in favor of both conversion and nurture to accomplish this task. Likewise the newly formed Christian Church (Disciples of Christ) encountered little resistance internally to the theology of choice, granting God's design in the decision-making process. On the other hand, deep splits occurred among Baptists, who moved from various theological traditions to unite only on sacramental and governmental grounds. A number of schisms plagued the Presbyterian and Reformed communions, as their Calvinistic heritage met the reality of changed lives and American optimism concerning society.

Episcopal and Lutheran communions, Roman Catholics, and to a certain extent even Jewish groups, were not so thoroughly affected by this particular theological question and not so dependent on the revival tradition in America. But each tradition still contended vigorously with its European roots and its American innovations.

Whole new communions arose to dislodge the traditions, sometimes having experienced counter-cultural life also in a European environment, as had the Rappites and at least a few of the Shakers. Sometimes, however, they countered the *textus receptus* (and the received canon for behavior as well) with new revelation, as in the case of the Church of Jesus Christ of the Latter Day Saints.

To make sense of these, not to mention the scores of other communions, some recounting of denominational stories is necessary. Some thematic generalizations might also help— such as assertions about the increasing parochialism of the period and the gradual externalization of religious drives—and these are made along the way. This chapter focuses on the communions present in strength at the time of the forming of the nation, and subsequent studies will explore in turn the new denominations and their derivatives.

Episcopal Recuperation

No communion had more power during the colonial years than did the Anglican Church. Belonging to the Established Church in Virginia, New York, Maryland, South Carolina, North Carolina, and Georgia, and to a "preferred" body in other colonies, Anglicans moved quickly from being "insiders" to becoming "outsiders" at the occasion of the Revolution. Anglican priests, who in the Southern colonies had frequently been less than paragons of piety, were sometimes discredited during that conflict, frequently accused of being spies, seldom successful in carrying out their ministrations, and almost always ambiguous in their sentiments regarding the Whigs. Clergy and laypeople alike had struggled to obtain an American bishop, a symbol to Anglicans of their acceptance as first class members in the Church of England, but a symbol to Puritans and disestablishment people of the American Anglican designs on their religious freedom.

Thus it was quite natural that the Episcopal Church suffered a significant decline as the Revolution bore fruit in an independent nation. But even in the face of disestablishment and the considerable antipathy of many Americans toward the Episcopal Church, the remnant managed to build a diocesan organization and to develop amazing warmness toward its new, free-church identity.

Leader in this new Protestant Episcopal Church, among others, was William White of Philadelphia (1747-1836). White, child of a wealthy landowning family, had likewise married into a family of wealth and prominence. He became rector of Christ Church, Philadelphia, during the Revolution and helped following the war to summon a convention organizing the new communion. Consecrated as a bishop by the Church of England in 1787 with Samuel Provoost, he helped reconcile various church factions by arranging the consecration of the first bishop on American soil, accepting the power of Samuel Seabury as being collegial although Seabury had himself received consecration only from the Scottish bishops. White was a member of the older school of Low Churchmanship, but did not foist that persuasion on the church. Subsequently, White served as presiding bishop from 1795 until his death.

Other bishops in American Episcopalianism's early years as an independent church were Thomas Claggett, Robert Smith, and Edward Bass. Historian William Manross has characterized their efforts as "cautious" ones, since they limited visitations and generally responded only to requests for assistance from local parishes.

In 1811, however, with the designation of John Henry

Hobart and Alexander Griswold as bishops, the Episcopal Church began a period of growth and development which has set its course in the U.S. until the present. Hobart (1775-1830), a protégé of White, graduated from the College of New Jersey in 1793. He served various churches in the Middle Atlantic states before becoming assistant pastor of New York's Trinity Church. His diocesan efforts, his writings and controversies thrust Hobart quickly into public view. In 1811 he was actually consecrated as an assistant bishop of New York, but immediately he began visitations and other work strengthening the church. By the time of his moving to become bishop, only five years later, the diocese had taken giant strides toward economic and spiritual health. Tireless in his efforts, Hobart personally confirmed 1100 persons during 1813 alone. His interests lay in the direction of Episcopal High Church solidarity, and he opposed the interdenominational benevolent enterprise, offering instead the beginnings of a denominational Sunday School board, an Episcopal Tract Society, and even a denominational Bible Society. He came to embrace the idea of a theological seminary for priests being in New York after initial opposition to it, and he aided the General Theological Seminary in achieving financial security. Later Hobart himself offered courses in pastoral theology and homiletics. In championing the High Church wing of the Protestant Episcopal Church, Hobart sought to reinforce the "wall of separation" between church and state, and he tried to unify the authority of the Prayer Book with that of the Bible.

Griswold (1766-1843), from an English-German family, had studied under his uncle Roger Viets, a missionary for the Anglican Society for the Propagation of the Gospel. Ordained a deacon by Seabury in 1795, and a priest during the following year, he proved a skillful minister in rejuvenating the Episcopal parish in Bristol, Rhode Island. This evident success led to his election as a bishop for the whole Eastern Diocese (incorporating almost all of New England).

He, with cooperation from clergy and laity, managed so to strengthen the diocese that after his death each state area itself offered the locus of a diocese. Griswold, in contrast to Hobart's views, esteemed experiential Christianity and increasingly became identified with the Evangelical wing of the church. He preached the import of personal conversion, scriptural authority, justification by faith, and numerous doctrines espoused in common by other Protestant communions. Griwold also sought common cause with other churches in the reform movement of his day—the causes of temperance, literacy, Bible printing and dispersion through a united Society, and recolonization of the slaves through the American Colonization Society. In the persons of Griswold and Hobart, the Low and High Church parties of the Protestant Episcopal Church began their traditions in this country, but both had in common an indefatigability which spurred denominational efforts and buttressed the work of priests, laypeople, and missionaries alike.

The Episcopal Church proved rather slow in moving westward. Philander Chase, an early missionary and first bishop consecrated for Ohio and Illinois, did manage to establish Kenyon College with Bexley Hall its attendant seminary. Chase's leadership methods proved so tyrannical, however, that he was soon forced to resign in 1831. Replaced in that diocese by C.P. McIlvaine, Chase continued his missionary service by organizing a diocese in Michigan (1832), and a distinct diocese for Illinois (1835).

Through the Domestic and Foreign Missionary Society of the Protestant Episcopal Church, organized in 1820, other missionaries were sent to Florida, and to the western states and territories. Although it began as a voluntary society, with annual dues for persons who joined, the Society was reorganized in 1835 to accentuate its denominational basis. By 1850, it managed as a mission wing of the church to have work underway in every state in the U.S., including the new one—California.

The Oxford Movement, with its celebrated series of Anglican conversions to Catholicism, had American repercussions. During the 1840's some graduates of the General Seminary became Catholics. Arthur Carey, also a graduate, confessed Tridentine theology even as the Bishop of New York, Benjamin Onderdonk ordained him. And one bishop, Levi Ives of North Carolina, actually converted to Catholicism while retaining his episcopacy. When brought to trial, he recanted temporarily, but in 1852 renounced Protestantism when he went to Rome. William Augustus Muhlenberg, Anglicized grandson of the famous Lutheran leader, led a "Memorialist Movement" in the church advocating new cross-class missions and worship experiences in an "evangelical Catholic" communion. For the most part, however, the ante-bellum Episcopal Church continued to suffer from what Manross termed "upperclassishness." The same could hardly be stated of the Methodist wing of Anglicanism, which developed during the period under present consideration.

Methodist Growth

Methodism, begun as a movement within Anglicanism, became a discernable denomination and a thoroughly popular one during the period under scrutiny. John Wesley had long ago visited America (1736-1738) and upon return to England experienced a heart "strangely warmed" at Aldersgate in May, 1738. With a similarly converted brother Charles, John Wesley led a religious upheaval. Careful religious discipline, "good singing," tight leadership, and small group ("class") identification led to the organization of Wesleyan societies throughout England and in a few colonies as well—American ones included. Methodist theology, and its concentration on human cooperation with divine grace, served Methodist ethics—living the Christian life and serving God wholly. The Christian life meant "ministry" for all who tried to live it.

Colonial Methodists, especially Irish and formerly German

groups in Maryland and New York, had tried as best they could to spread the word of Wesleyan faith. Robert Straw-bridge (d. 1781), Thomas Webb (1724-1796), and others had preached widely, organized societies, and strengthened the movement. On the eve of the Revolution, other Wesleyan preachers had arrived: people such as Joseph Pilmoor, Richard Broadman, Richard Wright and Francis Asbury. But although Strawbridge and others celebrated both Eucharist and Baptism, Wesley maintained that only ordained priests should administer either. Thus not until Wesley himself or-dained Richard Whatcoat and Vasey Elders, and Thomas Coke as superintendent for America, did the Church-being-born have an ordained ministry for leadership. With the Christmas Conference of 1784, and the designation of Coke and Asbury as bishops together with the ordination of nu-merous ministers, establishment of a juridical body to govern the church and oversee its development had occurred. Once organized in the new nation, Methodism flourished.

The doctrine, style of ministry, and general optimism of the Methodist Church commended that communion to the people of the American frontier especially. The circuit-riding preachers, called of God, could quickly move into ministry without lengthy apprenticeship demanded among some com-munions. Yet they did receive some training, and admoni-tions to learn as they practiced ministry. Likewise they could move quickly from congregation to congregation un-encumbered by the process of congregational assent to their ministry. In fact, the ideal preacher among the Methodists was a single person, ready to range broadly in serving many groups and visiting countless homes.

The Methodist circuit-rider accented human possibilities in responding to God's grace, divine love for all the audience, and the preferability of Methodism over other forms of worship and communion. There seems to have radiated from the preacher and layperson alike a confidence in the progress of the church that matched the political optimism of the

strapping nation. These sentiments were well-expressed by
Peter Cartwright, perhaps the best-known of the circuit-
preachers. Cartwright (1785-1872) served in frontier circuits
and locations in Kentucky, Tennessee, Ohio, and elsewhere
before finally settling in Illinois. Thus he spoke from experience in asserting:

> A Methodist preacher in those days, when he felt that
> God had called him to preach, instead of hunting up a
> college or Bible institute, hunted up a hardy pony of a
> horse, and some traveling apparatus, and with his li-
> brary always at hand, namely, Bible, Hymn Book, and
> Discipline, he started. . . . Often he slept in dirty cabins,
> on earthen floors, before the fire; ate roastingears for
> bread, drank butter-milk for coffee, or sage tea for
> imperial; took, with a hearty zest, deer or bear meat,
> or wild turkey, for breakfast, dinner, and supper, if he
> could get it. His text was always ready, "Behold the
> Lamb of God," etc.

Already by 1790, fourteen conferences were held in locations from Georgia to New York, with three of them west of
the Alleghenies on the new frontier. Almost 60,000 Americans belonged to the Methodist Church, and thousands more
called themselves "Methodists." Although Florida remained
closed to Protestants until 1820, all other of the Southern
states and territories received Methodism rather quickly and
rather thoroughly. Likewise another "missionary front"
moved Methodism westward into Kentucky and Indiana,
Ohio and Illinois, to focus Methodist growth on that frontier
as well.

Leaders among the Methodists, besides Peter Cartwright
the circuit-rider already mentioned, were indeed myriad.
What with its propensity for democratization and its propounding of the "whosoever will" doctrine of Christian
grace, local clergy and lay leaders did not suffer from the
"mystification process" that remained prevalent among some

groups of Episcopals and Reformed churchfolk. They took control of the church and developed it. However, despite the persons did stand out as bishops in the church—Francis Asbury and William McKendree.

Francis Asbury (1745-1816) came to America in 1771 specifically to preach the Methodist word after his own conversion to the movement in youth and some experience as a preacher in England. Imprisoned during the Revolution as a suspected Tory spy, he emerged after independence as a citizen of Delaware and a recognized leader. Asbury, with Thomas Coke, led the formative Christmas Conference and self-imposed the title of "bishop" (both its responsibility and authority) along with Coke. Autocratic in administrative style, he designated the circuits, assigned the preachers, called the conferences, and himself preached throughout the country, a living anomaly in the face of localization and democratization in the movement.

It is estimated that Asbury personally travelled 300,000 miles at least, mostly on horseback, preaching and exercising his episcopacy. Tall, skinny, and plainly dressed in a frock coat, Asbury in the saddle became a living symbol of the growing communion on the move.

Gradually Methodist power gravitated from Asbury to William McKendree, who himself was elected a bishop in 1808. McKendree (1757-1835), born in Virginia, had come to the ministry after service in the Revolutionary Army and some experience in Methodist societies. He took exception to Asbury's plan to concentrate church power in the hands of bishops, and he had separated briefly from the church with the defection of James O'Kelly and others at the time of their schism in 1792. O'Kelly would help form the Disciples of Christ, but McKendree drifted back to support Methodism and even to accompany Asbury on his rounds. Like Asbury, McKendree remained single and devoted himself especially to the southern and western societies, conferences, and missionaries. McKendree initiated such vital ingredients in American

Methodism as the church "cabinet," the episcopal address, and the educational emphases—himself donating six sections of land in Illinois to found the Lebanon Seminary.

Many Methodists began to practice their faith in the mainstream of American social and political life. Those whites who started on the fringe of society gradually became for the most part members of the middle-class. In the words of Cartwright, "the Methodists in that early day dressed plain; attended their meetings faithfully, especially preaching, prayer, and class meetings; they wore no jewelry, no ruffles...." Exercising temperance and discipline, they represented a new puritanism and reaped its economic rewards in addition to its spiritual ones.

But not all Methodists were white, and certainly black Methodists affirmed the inequities in U.S. society which permitted chattel slavery to flourish. Richard Allen and Harry Hoosier, both black Methodist preachers, had attended the Baltimore Conference of 1784. In 1799, Allen was ordained by Asbury having already been licensed to preach by St. George's Methodist Church in Philadelphia. White members and black had differing opinions of the meaning of the doctrine of the "communion of saints" in that situation, for white members of that congregation expected blacks to stay on the periphery of church life and blacks expected full participation. When relegated to a gallery in the church in 1787, blacks walked out with Allen and started another society. Allen himself remained a Methodist even when that congregation chose to become Episcopal. Despite Allen's attempts to work within Methodist structures, however, and despite his continuous friendship with Asbury, the schism occurred between black and white Methodists. The resultant branch of Methodism, Allen's African Methodist Episcopal Church, is the subject of another chapter, but this friction inculcated in vivid fashion the divided sentiments within the newly thriving communion as well as illustrating the problems of white acculturation typical for American religious communions that are predominantly white.

On a national scale, support and criticism of the institution of slavery caused a Methodist split in the year 1844. Actually, the O'Kelly group had totally opposed slavery and had injected into early Methodism certain anti-slavery presuppositions. As more Southerners joined the church, however, the sentiments of the denomination for a time changed to more neutral ones. Thus the General Conference of 1800, for example, still forbade a traveling preacher from holding slaves. But little attention was given to slavery until the 1840 Conference in which the subject permeated committee meetings and debating time on the floor as well. In the end, that Conference adopted what now appears to be a rather mild statement on the subject:

> The simple holding of slaves, or mere ownership of slave property, in states of territories were the laws do not admit of emancipation, and permit the liberated slave to enjoy freedom, constitutes no legal barrier to the election or ordination of ministers to the various grades of office known in the ministry of the Methodist Episcopal Church, and cannot, therefore, be considered as operating any forfeiture of right in view of such election and ordination.

The body had moved, seemingly, to embrace the institution of slavery, or at least to declare its moral neutrality. Anti-slavery Methodists, led by Orange Scott, withdrew three years later to form the Wesleyan Methodist Connection which based its separation on the matter of abolition, Methodist complicity in the evil of slavery. Others unwilling to split from the denomination moved within Methodist channels to reverse the statement at their next quadrennium.

The General Conference of 1844 suggested that bishop James O. Andrew of Georgia, a slaveholder, should cease to exercise his episcopal charge. Southerners, who refused to debate the matter of "ethics of slavery" on the floor of the 1844 General Conference, separated from the church to form the Methodist Episcopal Church, South. Yet another split occurred in 1859, 1860 when the holiness element withdrew, especially in the Genesee Conference, in part on the basis of their abolitionism.

Divide as they might, Methodists appeared to grow ever stronger in the years before the Civil War. They came to occupy center stage in American religion as the paradigmatic communion, an embodiment of the ideals and the shortcomings of the New World denominations.

Baptist Emergence

Sharing phenomenal growth patterns with the Methodists, Baptist communions swelled during the period under consideration to become indeed a plurality of the population in many areas of the United States. In Virginia, and from there migrating to Tennessee, Kentucky, and points south and west, Baptists moved with alacrity to encompass the frontier with congregations and associations. On the seaboard at times they continued to suffer ostracism and occasional persecution, but in the new states and territories they formed churches right and left. Winthrop Hudson, a provocative historian of American religion, argues that the Baptists made their greatest gains between 1789 and 1860 along the east coast.

American religious persecutions, generally stereotyped as a colonial phenomenon, were still occurring sporadically during the 1790's. Baptists in Barnstable and Yarmouth (on Cap Code) were taxed in January, 1790, for support of the Congregational ministers in those parishes. One tax collector took a horse from a non-complying Dissenter who owed less than $2. In states with established churches, Baptists were more frequently taxed, against their own theological stance, for support of their own pastors. And the subtle pressures to conform to "normal" religious practice in Virginia offered a negative invitation to them to resettle on the frontier.

During the 1800's, and perhaps due in part to lingering oppression of them, Baptists grew to become the most numerous among Protestant Christians. Baptist influence increased as their numbers grew. The more or less orderly growth of the denomination in early years, under the Philadelphia Baptist Association and its affiliates north and south, was superceded by a rather thorough autonomy on the part of local congregations and a proliferation of loose associations.

Time, and the intermingling of Baptist traditions, yielded a gradual dissolution of the various "Parties" among them— Regular Baptists, earlier a Reformed and Congregational group adhering to believer baptism; Separate Baptists, revivalistic and more internally oriented in community; General Baptists, English Arminian clusters; and Particular Baptists, Calvinistic and holding to a limited atonement. Many came even by the time of the Revolution to become believers in both predestination and free will. John Leland, for example, asserted that he concluded "that the eternal purposes of God, and the freedom of the human will, are both truths."

Leland, although not "typical" of Baptist ministers of the era, nevertheless presents a fine example personally of the causes for Baptist success. Born in Massachusetts in 1754, he devoted himself to the ministry early in life. He moved to Virginia, then to Kentucky and back to Massachusetts, seeking to pastor newly emerging flocks in the various states. He sought, during the Revolution and afterwards, to assure a constitutional separation of church and state, an end to the practice of chattel slavery, and other social goals. But he likewise sought to convert and baptize as many Americans as would follow Jesus. In his sparse *Journal*, Leland recorded the numbers and sometimes a description of the persons baptized—a total of more than 1500. In 1831, he also wrote a friend giving his impressions:

> I have seen a number of religious revivals within the limits of my ministration, and at this present time there is a shower falling in these parts. I have lately baptized forty, and others stand waiting. How it may appear to the solemn line of spectators, on the banks of the water, to

see an old man, whose locks have been frosted with seventy-seven winters, baptizing without any inconvenience, I cannot say; to himself there is a solemn pleasure.

Not all western Baptists were rejoicing to receive Baptist missionaries, however, and a strong anti-mission sentiment arose within the communion. It was not until some years after this feeling of sectional independence arose that the Primitive, or "Old School," Baptists organized to voice in concerted fashion their objections to missions (as well as their distaste for tract and Bible societies, denominational colleges and seminaries, Sunday Schools, and such). All these institutions designed by human hands were unbiblical and served to distance people from faith in God. Believers should rather focus on faith and scripture, on Christian life as God commanded them to do. Divine predestination, not human instrumentality, determined the elect.

A rudimentary form of this anti-mission spirit had preceeded the Black Rock, Maryland, meeting of 1832 by more than a decade. John Taylor of Kentucky had complained that missionary paradigms should come from scripture, not the reforming benevolent societies of the day. Likewise Daniel Parker of Illinois started a Two-Seed-in-the-Spirit Predestinarian Baptist Church, contending that Eve, for all creatures, carried two seeds imparted one by God and the other by Satan. Each person received one of these two seeds, destining the individual either for glory or perdition.

Most Baptists, however, continued in the mainstream of American evangelical Christianity as an amalgam theologically of predestinarian and Arminian views. Ministers, generally themselves farmers in the area, were licensed and usually ordained by the congregation in which they worshipped. Some, like John M. Peck, moved west to "call a church" after being baptized and ordained by a home congregation. Peck, mixing revivalism and covenant theology, periodically offered his flock the opportunity to give "an expression of their feelings, and their trials, hopes, aspirations, and joys."

In this time of covenant-renewal, Peck complimented his congregation for their "frankness and apparent sincerity."

The revival movements greatly increased the number of Baptists everywhere, but particularly in Kentucky. In 1790, Baptists numbered about 3000 in a total population of 73,000. Only 13 years later, there were 15,500. Though a huge number of Baptists joined the Campbellite exit to form the Christian Church, nevertheless Baptist conversions and confessions of faith more than offset the losses. Thus through the work of local ministers, lay people, and missionaries where they were meeting with receptive people, Baptist communions grew as diverse and autonomous units, holding in common only their antipedobaptism and their reliance on Biblical authority. Most agreed also on the necessity of church separation from state, and some even cooperated to establish seminaries and colleges. The autonomous nature of Baptist Churches affected neighboring communions as well, enabling a general American congregationalism that persists even among the connectional communions.

Reformed Denominations

Already in colonial and Revolutionary periods, Congregational and Presbyterian bodies had become quite strong in America. Indeed, the Puritan tradition has been considered determinative for the colonial experience by many scholars, and the War for Independence has been frequently termed "a Presbyterian Revolution." It might be argued that Reformed Christians actually instigated the American system of government. Parallels do exist between the organization of the U.S. government and the structure of Reformed judicatories. But Congregational bodies did not fare so well, comparatively, in the new nation; and the Presbyterians formulated a General Assembly only in 1789, a full five years after Methodist organization. A national identity had offered the context for a Presbyterian Assembly some years before one developed from the Synod system.

Congregationalists, many of whom were already inclined

to embrace connectional ties, formulated with the Presbyterians a Plan of Union in 1801. It provided for conjoint founding of new congregations and for amicable relations between those already existing. That plan remained in effect, allowing effortless transfer of ministers from one communion to the other and other reciprocal aids, for more than thirty years. Differing chiefly in matters of polity, the mainstreams of the communions were largely sharing an evangelical theology based on the Calvinism of the Westminster Standards. Problems arose, however, as the theology of the English interregnum met American voluntarism.

In 1775, Timothy Dwight had become President of Yale College, stronghold of Congregational Christianity in the new land. He began soon to preach forcefully on morality and evangelism, moving students and faculty alike to remember the Great Awakening and to embrace piety in the place of their perceived infidelity. Evidently Dwight's ministrations, and his calls for Christian conversion were well-received by all but the most recalcitrant of the covenant-directed persons; but as others began imitating Dwight, the question evolved quickly about how thoroughly the predestinarian focus of the Reformed faith could combine with revivalism. As Western Presbyterians proceeded in 1803 to ordain ministers committed to conversion, the problems were compounded.

Especially the Reformed church leaders remembered the mix of doctrines as they had arisen in the Great Awakening, when Jonathan Edwards had united theological strictness with preaching for conversion. As the fulcrum of the movement, Edwards had moved Calvinism into recommitment to the omnipotence of God, the power of predestination, and the finality of divine revelation. At the same time, he emphasized the sense of universal harmony toward accomplishing God's purpose for the world, divine benevolence, and a hope in progress among humankind. Many elements in the theology of the "Edwardeans" remained distinctly conservative—the primacy of Biblical authority, useful in testing all other forms of revelation; a rejection of the "self-determining power of the will," any dependence on human initiative for effecting salvation; an objective theory of the atonement; and a feeling of human responsibility for the results of sin. But the Edwardeans departed from the rigidity of earlier Calvinism regarding such doctrines as repentance, cooperating human ability, and the wrath of God.

One early formulation of Edwardean thought was by Samuel Hopkins (1721-1803), a graduate of Yale in 1741 and a personal protégé of Edwards himself. After losing one charge, Hopkins relocated in 1770 as minister of the First Congregational Church of Newport, Rhode Island. He remained there until his death. Hopkins also pioneered in denouncing slavery, a dangerous stance in a harbor town which profited greatly from the system.

Hopkins' *System of Doctrines* (1793), dwelled on the sovereignty of God and the Divine Will to good. "What great gratitude do we owe to God for giving such a complete revelation...!" he exclaimed. He also voiced the accompanying lament as well: "How very criminal and wretched are they who neglect or abuse this inestimable privilege of revelation from God!"

"Disinterested benevolence," the highest human motive, was for Hopkins the ethical goal for Christians. He recognized the natural propensity for people to regard "the interest and happiness of those who are nearest and most in sight more strongly and more tenderly" than those far away. However, the minister also encouraged "universal benevolence," a worldwide feeling of the "good of the whole." Christians should selflessly seek overall public interest over personal pleasures. God is concerned with all, he claimed; and people should be directed toward universal harmony in a god-like manner.

Universalism and Unitarianism—two rational extensions of this emphasis on God's goodness and human benevolence—appeared quickly with Reformed origins to challenge Edwardeanism as a "halfway measure." Especially the residual Calvinism in doctrines of the Trinity and the Atonement came under scrutiny. If overall good met God's intention, why should not beatitude universally apply? And if Christian authority was indeed Biblical, why then believe in the philosophical incursions on God's unity which were alien to the Testaments? Really now, was not "three in one" a rational absurdity, "bad arithmetic" in the words of Thomas Jefferson? Edwardean theology, with emphases on both Bible and reason, invited this reaction, too.

The challenge of Unitarianism proved the more thoroughgoing of the two. Harvard-educated for the most part, the liberal Congregationalists schemed to capture in 1805 the Hollis Chair in divinity at that college. Thus in the person of Henry Ware (1765-1845), formerly a pastor at Hingham, Massachusetts, Christian Unitarianism triumphed over Edwardean orthodoxy in the new nation's educational capitol. The conservatives reacted by founding a theological seminary they considered necessary in order to preserve trinitarian Reformed tradition— Andover Theological Seminary, the first such institution in the United States.

Andover as a seminary represented the union of old-line Calvinists and the Hopkinsian revisionists. The creed of the school, which professors there publicly affirmed each five years, included the following tenets:

I believe...that ADAM, the federal head and representative of the human race, was placed in a state of probation, and that, in consequence of his disobedience, all his descendents were constituted sinners;... that being morally incapable of recovering the image of his CREATOR, which was lost in ADAM, every man is justly exposed to eternal damnation. I moreover believe that GOD... hath foreordained whatsoever comes to pass, and that all beings, actions, and events, both in the natural and moral world, are under his providential direction; that GOD'S decrees perfectly consist with human liberty; GOD'S universal agency with the agency of man; and man's dependence with his accountability; that he has understanding and corporal strength to do all that GOD requires of him; so that nothing but the sinner's aversion to holiness prevents his salvation....

The creed mixed Calvinism and missionary confidence in the efficacy of conversion. It also brought new controversies as people like Moses Stuart, Professor of Sacred Literature at the seminary, saw no conflict between its theology and the appropriation of German Biblical criticism. The Trustees investigated Stuart in 1825, found that not only was he taking the teaching of biblical languages very seriously in classes (he translated from German the major portion of a Hebrew Grammar), but he was also employing the results of German critical research (such as those of Wilhelm deWette, in *A Critical and Historical Introduction to the Canonical Scriptures of the Old Testament*). Stuart was threatened but never dismissed, and he continued work until retirement in 1848. His intellectual honesty, together with the curiosity of others in the tradition, enabled a continual bridge between Reformed liberalism and Unitarianism even after the latter took its direction in the scientific humanism of Theodore Parker.

Meanwhile Universalism also encountered Calvinism. During colonial days, Charles Chauncy (1705-1787) had already preached universal salvation, sometimes opposing directly Edwards' predestinarian doctrines. But during the period under present consideration, Edwardeans themselves, such as Nathaniel Emmons (1745-1840) and Edward Griffin (1770-1837) flirted with atonement theologies that met their beliefs in the benevolence of God. Gradually a "governmental theory," dwelling on God's love, emerged. In Griffin's words, "A moral government wields all the motives in the universe.... It comprehends the atonement...and all institutions of religion." The step from such a comprehensive affirmation of God's purpose to a belief in God's universal salvific love of people was small indeed.

Specifically, Universalism beckoned Americans at the

beginning of the century through the ministry of Hosea Ballou (1771-1852), a former Baptist. The young man attended in 1791 the New England general Convention of Universalists and there began his preaching. As a Universalist missionary and circuit-rider he pioneered in the establishment of Universalist congregations and associations in New York and elsewhere. Later, as the pastor of Boston's Second Church, 1818-1852, he served as the primary voice of the movement.

Hosea's distant cousin, Adin Ballou (1803-1890), joined the Universalist Convention in 1823 but left in 1831 to form the Massachusetts Association of Universal Restorationists (dissolved in 1841). He likewise founded the Hopedale Community, in Milford, in that year, a consciously Christian utopian society (dissolved in 1856). Through the efforts of both Ballou cousins and their colleagues, Universalism remained a distinct challenge to orthodox Calvinism.

Both Unitarianism and Universalism, despite their centering in Boston, remained predominantly rural in flavor, and most adherents of these derivitives from Calvinism were farmers. A third movement out of Calvinistic Reformed communions was also rural in character, but Western in formulation—the Cumberland Schism.

To meet the needs of frontier Presbyterians, Transylvania Presbytery accepted for ministers (but did not yet ordain) four men who had no classical education. In 1802 Samuel King, Alexander Anderson, and Finis Ewing were licensed to preach over the objections of a minority of both ruling and teaching elders (both laypeople and ministers). Cumberland Presbytery, designated to include at this time a portion of the Transylvania territory, began to call and ordain preachers along the Baptist pattern, locating farmers who would be willing to shepherd flocks of their neighbors.

The intermediate judicatory for the area, the Synod of Kentucky, brought charges of heresy against Richard McNemar and John Thompson for holding alleged Arminian theologies and for preaching anti-Calvinist doctrines from their pulpits. Thus the educational dispute was joined with a theological one. Barton Stone and two other ministers met with McNemar and Thompson to form a new Presbytery of Springfield and to withdraw from the Synod. The highest Presbyterian judicatory, General Assembly, meeting in 1804, sought to heal breach and the five dissident ministers dissolved the Presbytery to form a whole new communion— variously called the New Lights, Reformers, and Stoneites. This communion too dissolved when Mr. and Mrs. McNemar along with members of their flock joined the Shakers, when Thompson and others rejoined the Synod, and when Stone moved toward union with the Campbellites.

But Cumberland Presbytery, investigated by Synod because of their "extremely defective" records of meetings, maintained the revivalistic wing of western Presbyterianism. In a complicated and questionable sequence of events involving the Presbytery, Synod, and General Assembly, revivalist members of the Cumberland faction were asked again to subscribe to the Westminster Standards. Ewing, King, and Samuel McAdow held out while others in the wing capitulated to the Synod's point of view. These three constituted the independent Cumberland Presbytery, the beginning of a separate communion. They accepted the confessions and discipline of the Presbyterians, rewrote their educational standards to make sense for the frontier, and adopted a form of Arminian-Calvinism to describe their belief in both free will and predestination. As their communion flourished, anti-revivalists came to regret their rejection of the Cumberland group.

Congregational bodies, with seemingly a built-in latitude for theological diversity in their very structure, were comparatively "safe" internally as heterodoxy from Calvinism whittled away at their edges. But Presbyterians found the theology of conversion and the ethics of America's slavery system attacking the very connectional basis in which they existed. The emerging New School of Presbyterianism embraced the paradox of conversion vs. predestination and Edwardeans led the way. Old School Presbyterians, however, resisted revivalism while holding a neutral position on the matter of slavery. The inevitable split occurred in 1837, ostensibly over theology alone. That the New School assemblies subsequently issued statements supporting anti-slavery while Old School assemblies issued several papers which justified slavery on biblical authority (the first in 1845) argues that tacit causes of the rupture included slavery sentiments.

Old School Presbyterians remained united north and south until 1861, months after Lincoln's Presidency had begun. Southern New School congregations (a definite minority in that communion) had withdrawn to form a separate structure in 1857. Both bodies exercised considerable influence in American social and political life during the first portion of the nineteenth century, and gradually Reformed communions increased with the growth of the nation and the augmentation in numbers of German and Dutch Reformed immigrants. Apparently an enormous amount of energy was internally consumed in these bodies, and bitter parochial quarrels took the place of more constructive activity a great deal of the time.

3

Strong, New Communions in America

Although the "inner-core" of evangelical communions in religious America remained unchanged during the period under consideration, strong inroads were made on its dominance by Lutherans, Catholics, Jews, and Disciples. The growing religious pluralism became apparent, to all including the most fervent and parochial believers of each.

Lutherans, of course, shared religious evangelicalism with the "established" Protestant communions. But the Germans and Scandinavians did not appear in numbers until after the Revolution. When they did, their religious ideas and belief structures underwent rather thorough realignment to accord with the free-church ethos already prevalent. They contended with many "internal" problems more than with direction of the government and the larger society during the times before the Civil War.

Catholics during this period were mostly Irish and German. They faced a predominantly French leadership pattern in America. Again, they did participate in the national life of the country, but for most of the time, most of the areas, it was from the "outside looking in." Their questions within the church stemmed from the peculiar American environment and untried governmental patterns. But during the antebellum years, American Catholicism explored the various avenues that would predominate in later eras.

It was during these decades that American Jews also came and set the patterns of religious observance that would characterize their later experiences also. Precious few had been in the U.S. at its inception, and during the first part of the nineteenth century they immigrated in increasing numbers. Though the "nativism" which discouraged their settling in various communities was sometimes more subtle than the anti-Catholicism, the Jewish people too shared in Protestant anti-foreign reactions—they were also victims of American prejudice.

A number of Protestants formed the Disciples of Christ, which though it shared tenets of several communions began to confront all of them with threatening anti-creedalism. Though they, as Jewish, Catholic, and Lutheran Americans later came to share religious enfranchisement in the nation, Disciples during this period were "outsiders" for the most part.

Lutheran Organization

Lutheranism, of course, had been present in colonial America due to Swedish, German and Dutch immigrants. Its growth to become a major force in the religious development of the U.S., however, occurred during the ante-bellum years. According to most scholars, the direction of American Lutheranism had been first established by Henry Melchior Muhlenberg (1711-1787), who focused the German-Americans especially on synodical organization, the opportunities of the frontier, and the possibilities of Lutheranism flourishing in a "free-church" environment.

Early Lutherans in the Ministerium of New York cast their religious lot with the newly emerging Protestant Episcopal Church in the U.S.A. They saw much in common between the communions' theology and worship practices. They established a comity arrangement with the Episcopalians, and they adopted English as the official language of the church in 1807. Meanwhile more conservative members in the Pennsylvania Ministerium prevailed, insuring temporary affirmation of German as the continuing language of worship and seeking whatever rapproachment occurred with Reformed bodies rather than with "Anglicans," whom they categorized as Rationalists.

Gradually formal Lutheran organization grew also in North Carolina, Ohio, Maryland, Virginia, and Tennessee. In 1820 Lutherans formed a General Synod, but few of either the left or the right wings cared at first to join. Samuel Schmucker (1799-1873), a pietist and ecumenist, managed to widen the support of the Synod. A graduate of Princeton, Schmucker found common cause with other evangelicals of differing denominations in seeking to concentrate on the task of "Christianizing" the nation. He termed denominational differences "peculiarities," and considered that "these peculiarities" were not "equal in importance with the great fundamentals of our holy religion held in common by all." Schmucker also founded Gettysburg seminary in 1826 to train American pastors in the Lutheran tradition.

Increasingly strength came to the Lutheran communions through immigration from Germany and the Scandinavian countries. Some of the newcomers were Catholic, but more were from Lutheran areas. More than 1,500,000 Germans came to the U.S. between 1800 and 1860, the great majority settling finally in the North and West. Even with additions, however, the Synod never operated as a higher judicatory so much as it existed for advising and coordinating efforts in the various areas where Lutheranism was growing.

"Americanization" was largely taken for granted as a Lutheran tendency. Questions arose, naturally, concerning the extent to which changes in the new nation were appropriate for the communion. Schmucker moved, for example, to embrace increasingly the voluntary reform efforts in concert with Methodists, Presbyterians, Congregationalists, and others. He did so in the name of Lutheranism. He also professed a belief in the eucharistic doctrine of "spiritual presence," much as the Calvinists articulated it. Thus he evidenced departure from the traditional Lutheran position of "consubstantiation," as Luther himself had formed it. On the other hand, Professor Charles Philip Krauth soon called Lutherans "back to our father's house," requesting strict adherence to the Augsburg Confession and other catechetical bases of the traditional faith. Most of the argument focused on an American recension of the Augsburg Confession, sought and formulated by Schmucker and Benjamin Kurtz, among others. The General Synod did not adopt the new theology, as widely differing portions of the Synod voted it down. However three geographical territories in Ohio, parts of Indiana, and other scattered groups under the influence of Kurtz, did adopt it. Most Lutherans chose instead to remain confessionally and linguistically tied to their continental homeland, while adopting a "free-church" stance regarding U.S. church-state relations. This consistency in traditionalism would force denominational splits in years to come; but for the moment it produced only a paralysis of the National Synod and a few bodies of dissenters.

Real denominational strength lay in the complex pattern of geographical synods, many of which overlapped with other such bodies geographically. The internal organization of Lutheranism was extremely complicated, with a Melanchthon Synod of Americanizers splitting from the Maryland Synod and aligning with like-minded Lutherans elsewhere, for example.

On the frontier, irregular patterns of worship and religious behavior were to be found, horrifying the traditionalists. Some of the congregations held revivals and camp meetings despite warnings from the east to avoid these avenues of religious excess. As German immigration brought new strength to American Lutheran bodies, it also brought orthodoxy to the west in the person of C.F.W. Walther (1811-1887), and in the rise of the Missouri Synod he helped to organize. Walther asserted the responsibility and authority of local congregations to call pastors, and he led in the founding of a school of theology in St. Louis to produce ministers with such a commitment to limited local autonomy. Missouri Synod Lutherans overlapped geographically with the Iowa Synod and Wisconsin (originally Buffalo) Synod as well.

Norwegian Lutherans began arriving in Wisconsin in large numbers during the 1830's. Most were "low-church" Lutherans, with limited liturgy and strong preaching as religious preferences. These Scandinavians found that their sentiments aligned them with the Missouri Synod, and they established a professorship of their own at St. Louis in the seminary. They likewise cooperated in sending missionaries among the Indians. A portion of the Norwegian fellowship formed the Eielsen Synod, named for Elling Eielsen (who was himself discharged from the Synod he led after an ecclesiastical uprising in 1848). Others formed the Synod for the Norwegian Evangelical Lutheran Church in America. Repeated splits plagued the denominations throughout the ensuing decades.

Swedish Lutherans organized their first mid-American congregation in 1848, soon receiving the services of the Reverend Lars P. Esbjörn of the Swedish Missionary Society. Pastor Esbjörn led the growing Swedish population toward joining the Northern Illinois Synod as it began in 1851, but when he moved to Chicago the Swedish-Americans withdrew to assist in organizing the Augustana Synod with a number of Norwegian Lutherans.

All in all, growing confessionalism characterized the Lutherans during this period. It was for them a time of retrenchment from the ecumenism of former decades. The conservative wing of Lutheranism was consistently gaining in strength while American Lutheranism diminished in ecumenical influence.

Catholics

On August 15, 1790, Father John Carroll was consecrated in England as the first Roman Catholic bishop for the U.S. He assumed his responsibilities in Baltimore during December, and about one year later held the first synod on November 7, 1791.

Although Carroll's appointment represented the establishment of a first See, Catholics already had more than 24,500 communicants in the various states of the Union at the time of his assuming office. Moreover thousands of Catholics lived elsewhere in the territory that would become a portion of the U.S. In 1795, Father Luís Ignacio Maria de Peñalver y Cardenas (1749-1810) arrived in New Orleans as another American bishop, related to Spanish colonies in Louisiana and Florida. He, like Carroll, recognized that though vast opportunities existed in America for Catholic missions, at present a spiritual apathy existed among the faithful. "The inhabitants do not listen to, or if they do, they disregard, all exhortations to maintain in its orthodoxy the Catholic faith," he complained. Only among the Ursuline nuns could Bishop Cardenas find any evidence of solid education for Catholic growth and development (in this case, for women). Alas! The Ursulines maintained a pro-French bias.

But strongly religious Catholics began immigration from European countries to the U.S. at a rate unprecedented in the history of the Church. They came from Germany and Ireland, for the most part, but also they migrated from France and Italy, not to mention English Catholic families from time to time. By the 1790's 3000 black Catholics (both slave and free) lived in Carroll's See. With mission efforts, this Afro-American Catholic population increased somewhat. Statistically, however, and in terms of leadership, the "new" Americans accounted for Catholic vitality during these ante-bellum decades.

To Irish and German Catholics it seemed that French prelates were in control of the Church during the first part of the nineteenth century. In fact, Ambrose Marechal effectively succeeded John Carroll (not counting the brief interlude of aged Leonard Neale), as bishop of Baltimore. Benedict Flaget became bishop of Bardstown, Kentucky. Jean Dubois was made bishop of New York, and William Du Bourg served as the new bishop of New Orleans. Thus with their leadership, and that of numerous other French priests, the reality met the appearance of Gallic control. The accusation had basis in truth.

With the rise in numbers and responsibilities of Irish priests American Catholicism began reflecting its composition ethnically in its heirarchy. Foremost among the early Irish bishops was John England (1786-1842), consecrated and appointed to an American See in South Carolina in 1820. England, a native of Cork, where as a member of a Catholic minority as he grew up, he had already learned to contend with hostile majorities in religious and political matters. England had achieved considerable renown as a preacher, writer, and reformer by the time he arrived in America. In the newly created diocese of South Carolina, England broached and resolved temporarily the problem of Catholic lay trusteeship in the new nation. In American Catholic parishes, laypeople had held title as trustees to church property. Sometimes they even exercised a dubious power (by Catholic standards) of calling and dismissing priests. Carroll's tacit approval of the system meant that the powers accorded to bishops were sometimes proving exceedingly tenuous. To Irish parishioners in Virginia and elsewhere, this trusteeship had offered a countervailing power to the French prelates' priestly authority. Now England simply instituted a vestry program patterned after the Episcopal one—his constitution gave the bishop final power over finance in each parish, but it allowed for lay consultation and occasionally participation in the process of making decisions. Rome finally disapproved England's attempt at reconciliation between American and Catholic traditions.

Another major area where England made a valiant attempt to bridge human chasms in understanding was in his efforts to foster a climate of acceptance among Protestants for their

Catholic neighbors. Thus he spoke frequently at public lec-
tures and he often preached at Protestant churches when invited to share in worship. He argued forcefully that Catholic
ecclesiology could agree totally with American democratic
ideals. In front of the Congress of the U.S. (a thoroughly
Protestant body), England attested that he "would not allow
to the Pope, or to any Bishop" the right to "the smallest inter-
ference with the humblest vote at our most insignificant bal-
lot box." England's accommodationism was lost, for awhile,
when following his death few Catholics sought to build upon
his peace-making efforts with American politics and folk-
ways of the Protestant majority.

By the same token, American Protestant nativism arose
during the same period to threaten Catholics and to help
snuff out possibilities for harmony and active cooperation
between devotees of both religious flavors. At England's
urging a Provincial Council of Catholicity in America had
met in Baltimore in 1829. But their decrees did nothing to
ease fears on the part of Protestants that "Romish designs" on
the U.S. were being carried out to end the rights of freedom
of worship in the new country. Among the 38 statements
were warnings about "corrupt [Protestant] translations of the
Bible" and pleas to save the coming generations of Catholic
children from perversion by establishing parochial schools.

Protestants, with already a regrettable history during colonial and Revolutionary times of oppressing Catholic minorities, began a campaign to eliminate the "menace of
Popery." George Bourne initiated in 1830 a new periodical
(the first of many nativist publications), *The Protestant*. His
avowed intent was "to inculcate Gospel doctrines against
Romish corruptions." Bourne's hard core nativism did not
prove so popular as he and various backers had supposed.
The soft core approach of subsequent editors brought success
in 1834, however, and set the stage for a verbal exchange that
persisted throughout the remainder of the century.
Organizationally W. L. Brownlee formed the New York

Protestant Association, following the example of other "reform" enterprises in its voluntary style. Debates raged between him and other nativists on the one side and the Reverend John Hughes, a priest in Philadelphia and other Catholics on the other. "No-Popery" monographs, imported from England, found a good market in America. And the war of words increased in intensity.

Finally words incited action when the famed Calvinist Lyman Beecher returned from Cincinnati to Boston in the midst of a brouhaha involving a "nun escapee" who although allegedly "recaptured" by the Ursuline sisters, was actually confirmed to be again content in the order house. Nevertheless Beecher produced anti-Catholic sermons in three Protestant churches on a Sunday night. On the following night a mob of Protestants sacked and burned the Ursuline school at Charlestown, Massachusetts. They engaged in the first concerted act of nativist violence, a foretaste of many and even more brutal deeds to come. Rumors that Irish reprisals were planned brought further burnings and threats of personal harm to Catholics in the area.

Popular reaction to nativist mob activity across the country amounted to support of the Boston Protestants for "their use of questionable means to a good end." Rioters arrested were acquitted at their trials, and many Bostonians celebrated the anniversary of the burning a year later. More scandalous anti-Catholic tracts appeared, notably *Six Months in a Convent* by Rebecca Theresa Reed and Maria Monk's *Awful Disclosures of the Hotel Dieu Nunnery of Montreal*, pornography of the day in religious garb. Nevermind that both were answered in a mature fashion, the movement fed upon itself and generated interest in the passing of new laws governing Catholic immigration. Protestant invectives focused on the parochial school system, the perceived Catholic conspiracy to take the U.S. from the west, and on recent Catholic gains through democratic processes. Know-Nothingism, led in part by Charles Allen and his

Order of the Spangled Banner (an elaborate hierarchy of nativist ballyhoo in the form of a secret society), passed through the political sky of the 1850's like a giant meteor. The aim of Know-Nothingism was to place Protestant anti-Catholics in all political offices. In 1854, it gave promise of real success. Republican victories, compounded by Know-Nothing disasters in governing, brought the party to a screeching halt soon afterward. Know-Nothing political direction, like the earlier tracts and riots, aimed in large measure at making life miserable for the members of Catholic religious orders.

Misguided though they were, nativists did perceive correctly that the religious orders offered Catholicism a source of strength in the nation to which nothing in Protestantism was comparable. Early bishops Marechel, Du Bourg, Flaget, and many others had been members of the Society of Saint Sulpice. Efforts by Sulpicians were matched only by those of Jesuits in the early life of Catholic America. The Jesuits even continued to function effectively, though unofficially, during the time of their dissolution as an organized religious body. Members of religious orders brought a mobility and dedication to the task of Christianizing the new country which enabled them to move quickly and decisively into new territories with considerable resources to sustain their work.

The first religious congregation initiated in and for the U.S., the Sisters of Charity of St. Joseph, was founded by Elizabeth Bayly Seton (1774-1821). Mother of five and a convert from the Protestant Episcopal Church after the death of her husband in 1803, she opened a school for girls in Baltimore in 1808. With four companions she founded a religious community to serve the school. Mother Seton's order, with its headquarters soon moved to Emmitsburg, Maryland, opened the earliest American parish school, in Philadelphia. Already by the time of her death, Mother Seton's Congregation was aiding widely in parochial education and with other matters of health and spiritual growth for the whole church.

Other religious orders, imported from various countries

for special work, included Dominicans, Franciscans, and Benedictines. They came to serve in a variety of ways the needs of new American Catholics.

In 1853, at the very height of the nativist movement, Archbishop Cajetan Bedini visited the U.S. to report on American Catholicism. He found that approximately 2,000,000 Americans, about 9% of the population was Catholic. He cited the still pressing needs for better education among them, the suggestion of an office for information in the country to combat Protestant slander, and he expressed strong admiration for the American Catholics, struggling against odds to situate peaceably in the cities and farms of the nation. By the time of the Civil War, Catholics had overcome much, if not most, of the blatant Protestant antipathy expressed during the decades under scrutiny.

American Judaism

Until the Revolutionary era, no rabbis led synagogues in America. At least nine of the thirteen colonies to secede are known to have had one among the Jewish people in them. Services in congregations at Charleston, Newport, New York, and Philadelphia—wherever ten adult males could gather as a *minyan*—were led by the *hazzan*, or prayer service pastor. A subsequent *hazzan*, Isaac Leeser (1806-1868), first preached an English sermon in an American synagogue. He also translated the Hebrew Bible, Ashkenazic and Sephardic prayerbooks into English. But until 1836, the American Jewish population remained tiny—perhaps limited to a minority of the cities, with precious few Jewish families among the nation's rural majority.

German Jews, experiencing persecution and economic depression in their homeland, began migrating in wholesale fashion during 1836. Their entry into the mainstream of American life, as well as their occupying the ethnic ghettos of several cities, radically changed the religious life of the nation. As many as 150,000 Jews lived in the U.S. in 1860.

Almost all of the incoming Jews were orthodox in their

religious commitment. Reform Judaism arose in rather spontaneous ways, although some immigrants brought Reform tendencies from the German synagogues. The first congregational evidence of the Reform movement was in the shortening of services, the preaching in English, and the incipient "modernized" doctrines expressed in Charleston, South Carolina, in 1824. Isaac Harby led in the formation of a "Reformed Society of Israelites," a group that worshipped with the help of musical instruments and mixed liturgical use of English with the Hebrew.

Reform strength grew in that city until the innovation party assumed leadership of the Congregation Beth Elohim, the synagogue from which the Society had split, in 1840. The Reverend Gustav Poznanski, a Polish Jew with considerable experience in Germany, became their minister. During the 1840's, a number of congregations followed suit in other cities, either splitting from the established synagogues or organizing new ones in places like Baltimore, New York, Chicago, and elsewhere.

Without doubt the rabbi who most influenced American Jewish reform was Isaac Mayer Wise (1819-1900), who emigrated from Radnitz, Czechoslovakia, to New York in the year 1846. He had studied the Reform movements in Germany, and he sought consciously to implement what he had learned about them as the rabbi of the traditionalist Congregation Beth-El of Albany, New York. He began to preach in English, to mix the men and the women both in seating for worship and in the singing. He tried also to increase the rights of women in congregational government. He argued to Jewish colleagues in the U.S. that a national organization of Reform bodies was very much needed in order to train rabbis, to provide resources for worship, and to meet other common needs.

Wise moved to Cincinnati in 1853 as the rabbi of Congregation Bene Yesherun. There he began to publish two periodicals, *Die Deborah* in German and *The Israelite* (later *The*

American Israelite). In these periodicals, and in speeches and letters to friends, Wise disseminated his ideas about reform, in which he sought to retain the "essential" portions of Judaism while changing those parts inimical to American life. Wise termed his program "liberal," "progressive," "universal," "rational," and "practical."

In 1855, Wise convened in Cleveland the first national conference of rabbis, inviting both Orthodox and Reform Jews. The compromise statement, adopted at that conference, identified the middle ground on which very few of the participants stood; but it showed they could constructively meet, and agree to disagree: "The Bible, as delivered to us by our fathers and as now in our possession, is of immediate divine origin and the standard of our religion. The Talmud contains the traditional, legal, and logical exposition of the biblical laws, which must be expounded and practiced according to the comments of the Talmud."

The statement, and ensuing exchanges among the rabbi's of the various points of view, helped identify points of Jewish solidarity; and they helped to isolate areas of friction as well. Wise also published, as a result of the Cleveland Conference, an *American Rite* (Minhag), a predecessor of the *Union Prayer Book.*

David Einhorn, (1809-1879), another formulator of Reform Judaism in the U.S., came from Germany and Hungary to be the new rabbi of the Congregation Har Sinai of Baltimore in 1855. It was he who helped to move Reform thought to consider the corporate messiahship exercised by the Jewish people, a reinterpretation of not only the Suffering Servant imagery in Isaiah and elsewhere, but of the state of the Jewish nation as well. Were the people of God still in exile, to be restored in a geographic nation promised to their forebearers? Or were they rather the nation already restored to their inheritance? Einhorn stood for the cogency of the latter hermeneutic. He took exception with the methodology and interpretations of scripture which Wise had popularized, and he accused Wise of "pusillaminity" and of faltering logic in establishing a half-hearted reform. But Einhorn cooperated in the concerted movement for a standardizing of Reform Judaism in America. First in Baltimore and then in Philadelphia at Keneseth Israel Congregation (1861-1866) and finally with Congregation Adath Jeshurun (1866-1879) Einhorn kept his Reform theories in constant practice, moving through local innovations to consider the more general ones for U.S. Jews.

Some Jewish scholars, notably Ellis Rifkin of Hebrew Union College among others, claim that American Judaism developed hand in hand with the nation's capitalistic economic system. Thus the support of individualism, a climate for innovation and the protection of personal rights, and the spirit of competition in America fed a sense of toleration and respect for differing peoples who functioned well in such an atmosphere. Rifkin, presumably would differentiate the tacit anti-Semitism prevalent in American nineteenth century society from the blatant anti-Catholic behavior of the American nativists, who never attacked Jews so forcefully as they did "Papists" in their misguided sense of reform.

Most scholars, however, credit the Jewish people with discerning an American spirit of tolerance in religious matters, and suiting their social and economical life to the climate of that American "freedom," limited though it was. Already by the time Jews arrived in numbers in the U.S., Protestants had forced from each other these "freedoms," although they had not yet been extended to include Indian, black, or even white female inhabitants. Thus Jews benefitted as the general "freedoms"—worship, speech, vote, etc.—extended more deeply into American society. Moreover they began actively to undertake the broadening of these privileges to include American minorities sensing their own solidarity with those people.

Disciples of Christ
The first thorough ecumenical movement in American

Protestantism resulted, ironically, in the formation of yet another major denomination—the Disciples of Christ, or Christian Church. The movement toward the new communion stemmed in part from frontier voluntarism, but in particular it grew from at least four distinct groups of Christians.

The "Stonites," followers of Barton Stone (1772-1844), had been New Light Presbyterians. Under the guidance of Stone and others, six pro-revival ministers and a number of adherants had formed the Springfield Presbytery in 1803 when traditionalists among the Presbyterians refused to recognize the special needs of the frontier people and likewise refused to grant their requests for innovative standards for ministers. The Stonites embraced an open Arminianism—a focus on human ability to choose God's grace and accept it. Although some of the New Lights, as we have already seen, subsequently joined the Shakers and others returned to Presbyterianism, a large number of Kentucky "Christians" looked to Stone for leadership, and to congregational polity for church government.

The "O'Kellyites," too looked to a restoration of the simple gospel as a basis for Christian communion, and they also sought an end to creedal division among Christians. From the Methodist Episcopal Church, as Bishop Asbury was developing it, they moved to separate themselves and to form a new communion under the leadership of James O'Kelly (1735-1826) and Rice Haggard. O'Kelly had been elected and ordained an elder at the time of the organization of the Methodist Episcopal Church, in 1784. As a member of the first Council, or governing body before the beginning of the General Conference, he opposed Asbury. As the latter began exercising his episcopal title and prerogatives, O'Kelly organized a Republican Methodist Church dedicated not to episopacy but to more representative governmental structures. Before long, however, its members called themselves "Christians." Likewise an anti-Calvinist "Christian Connection" arose and began repudiating Baptist theology while embracing such a form of government.

Some scholars describe all three of these movements as "incipiently Unitarian"; and they name other such "swarmings" of frontier people that also contributed to the Christian Church. But these all coalesced around yet another "Christian" group which proved to become the center of the Disciples movement.

The "Campbellites" formed a fourth strand in the making of the Christian Church. They acknowledged Thomas Campbell (1763-1854) and his son Alexander (1788-1866) as founders of the movement. It was Thomas Campbell's statement," Where the Scriptures speak, we speak; where the Scriptures are silent, we are silent," which became a guiding principle for the Disciples. The two ex-Presbyterians and their colleagues worked first in establishing the Brush Run, Pennsylvania, Church. It, in turn, helped form numbers of other congregations in the Christian Association.

Disciples believed that lay people, underemphasized in the Presbyterian form of government and theology, should have a large part in governing the church. At first their efforts appeared "Baptist," because they immersed believing adults and self-consciously employed the term "Baptist" in describing their work. However they moved from such a self-labeling and left the Baptists to form the Christian Church in 1832. By 1835 most of the congregations in the four streams described had already decided to join the new communion. Very rapidly the new denomination spread, as Alexander Campbell and others of its leaders moved through the frontier preaching and evangelizing.

Alexander Campbell himself edited *The Millenial Harbinger*, a popular periodical, for over three decades. There he expounded the theology and worship of the emerging church. He spoke of faith, declaring that "there is no true and real conflict between faith and reason." Rather the two worked together in God's summoning people to himself, and teaching them to live with each other. Campbell spoke of the Bible, saying "it is the word of God," a "specific embodiment of the

Holy Spirit." He likewise told Christians how to worship, and he arranged in *The Christian System*, a separately published volume, ideas first explored in periodical.

The Christian System, published in 1836, offered a theological and liturgical guide for the new body. It called on believers to concentrate on salvation by faith alone. It asserted that "the one fact is expressed in a single proposition—*that Jesus the Nazarene is the Messiah.*" The System also proceeded to set priorities on Christian observance, declaring that baptism is "the one institution" for the church. "Wrong sacramental theology," however, did not disqualify the Christian from membership in the communion if that person had faith in Jesus' Messiahship. However Campbell did argue contentiously on the basis of biblical evidence the value of the new denomination and the shortcomings of other interpretive traditions.

Most of all, Campbell argued in winsome fashion with all comers—a popular debating style in the pre-television years would almost always draw a crowd. As the exponent of believer baptism he contended with N. L. Rice. As the champion of Protestantism, he debated against the Catholic Bishop John B. Purcell; and he played on the anti-Catholic feelings of many Americans to further his movement. And as the protector of Christendom against anarchy and free love, he "fought" Robert Owen in Cincinnati, Ohio in 1829.

Immensely popular personally, Campbell influenced political and religious attitudes of Americans as he bolstered his particular brand religion. He fought for emancipation of Virginia's slaves, for example, as a member of that state's Constitutional Convention in 1829. He likewise lent support to theological reforms, and helped Presbyterians among others become more aware of the narrowness of their traditional trinitarianism. Mostly, though, he cajoled and argued, prayed and preached the new communion into a real position of strength.

Early figures for membership in the denomination are difficult to find. In 1860, they numbered about a quarter million in the actual Christian (Disciples) denomination, although Alexander Campbell, always thinking inclusively and optimistically of his attempt at Christian unity, had estimated that at least that many Americans were members of the church long before that time. As a denomination committed to bringing all Christendom together "in the style of the New Testament Church," Disciple ministers and laypeople had no qualms about persuading members of other "devisive, creed-serving" splinter groups such as the Methodists and Presbyterians to join them instead.

Of course, the faithful members of those bodies took a rather dim view of Disciples proselyting from among their number. They thus considered the Disciples Church as spiritually threatening; and since the professed creeds the Disciples considered extra church baggage, mainstream communions regarded Christians as theologically reductionistic. Thus in many western communities the growing good will between mainstream Protestant congregations stopped short of including the Christians.

During the period under consideration, the Disciples Church was not for the most part a mainstream communion. It moved as an heuristic force into new frontier areas—Indiana, Texas, Illinois, and elsewhere. Discipline strength remained essentially west of the Alleghenies, except that churches earlier influenced by the Campbells and O'Kelly sometimes joined. Therefore the denomination differed from other Protestant bodies, which had lingering leadership on the seaboard even as the frontier moved across the plains. Disciples differed also in that they did not organically divide at the occasion of the War of Southern Secession. For one thing, Campbell had been anti-slavery from the time of his initiating the movement. In addition, large degrees of autonomy meant that even a denominational word during the war in support of the Union was evidently taken by southern Disciples as just a necessary and uneventful appeasement of the federal authorities. Such solidarity led Disciple minister Moses E. Lard to rejoice, prematurely, that "We can never divide." Divide they did, but the schism came after the period under present consideration.

4

The Communitarian Reaction

The early 1800's offered not only incredible growth patterns for most denominations and the rise of some new communions, they also saw the establishment of scores of religious utopian communities in America. German pietists, left-wing reformers, millenialists, philosophers, come-outers, revivalists, and a host of others set up communes to incarnate their espoused life-styles.

At present but five of these differing community patterns will be observed—the Shakers, the Rappites, Oneida, Brook Farm, and the Mormons. Each of these communitarian movements, however, is representative of a whole series of such efforts. The Society of the Public Universal Friend resembled the Shakers; Zoar, Bethel, and the Swedish Bishop Hill Community were similar to the Harmonist commune.

Most nineteenth century American communitarian movements began with a charismatic leader or family, and disciples joined in direct or vicarious identification with that person or group. All had in common a reaction to the general thrust of American nineteenth century economics, and their communal social life was a countervailing ideology against the rampant individualism in American society. One visitor's comments on the New Harmony Rappites and their neighbors reflects the power of this threat:

At first the people, for a great distance around the Settlement, being supplied with goods they could not easily procure elsewhere, considered it advantageous to them; but they now think precisely the contrary; for the Harmonites, not having to pay their workmen, are enabled to under-sell everyone who would wish to set up a store, and thus prevent competition. Moreover, as in exchange for their clothes, linens, hats, whiskey, etc., they receive vast sums of money which they never spend, and thus diminish the circulating medium of the country. (sic)

With hostile neighbors in American mainstream religion, few of the communal experiments survived the deaths of their founders, and fewer still made the necessary adjustments to technology and American lifestyle that permitted survival for later periods. The Church of Jesus Christ of the Latter Day Saints, most successful of the communitarian movements in terms of numbers of adherents, had already moved by the time of the Civil War into a pattern of life closer to that of an American denomination than to that of an intentional commune. The Shakers also managed to continue, after a fashion, into the present century. Brook Farm disbanded during the period under scrutiny. And the Rappites and Oneidans continued through the century in a drastically altered and comparatively spiritless manner. Had Americans in general provided graciousness and good will undergirding the experiments....? The results can only be a matter of speculation.

Communes bridged the dichotomy between frontier and seaboard in nineteenth century America. The Rappites even moved back eastward at the very time that western migration was in full force (1824). Shaker societies were practically interchangeable, except for a few varying production techniques and products, whether they existed in Massachusetts or Kentucky. In this respect they also offered a difference from the "normal" American way of life in the era.

Altogether the communitarian experiments offer a fascinating (yet rather unrepresentative) view of American religion in the period between Revolution and Civil War.

Shaker Life

Strictly speaking, Shakerism began in England with Ann Lee's membership in the left-wing Quaker group led by Jane and James Wardley. For all practical purposes, though, Shakerism belongs to the American experience. Millenial, convolutionary "French Prophets" brought forth in the industrializing cities of Britain, especially in Lancaster, pietistic cell groups such as the Wardleys' "Shaking Quakers." But America's incipient utopianism of the post-Revolutionary period offered Mother Ann and her colleagues space "to praise God in songs and dances." America afforded Mother Ann herself considerable harassment, but also the promise of a flourishing church by the time of her death in 1784.

Daughter in the family of a British blacksmith, Ann Lee received almost no formal education and worked from a very young age—in a cotton factory, as a cook, in the cutting of fur, and in numerous other menial occupations. In 1758 she joined the Wardleys. Together they focused on various types of religious activity and speculation—prophesies, signs, confession, and millenial longings. Married, also to a smithy, Ann gave birth to four children who all died in infancy. She considered herself guilty—depraved—because she engaged in sexual intercourse with her husband. And she deemed that God's punishment was upon her in the tragic loss of her children.

As her sentiments intensified, her religious activities became the more fervent—and the more radical. Placed in jail for "disturbing the peace." Ann experienced divine revelation. She began to speak in tongues, to preach the sinfulness of marriage, and to lead the newly emerging society as "Mother Ann," the female incarnation of the Messiah, Jesus of Nazareth.

Obeying a heavenly vision, she immigrated to New York in the summer of 1774 with her small company—her husband Abraham Standerin, two other members of the Lee family, and five believers. Her husband separated from her in 1775, and Mother Ann moved a bit later to a farm near Albany with the faithful remnant of her little groups. At Niskeyuna she formed "The United Society of Believers in Christ's Second Appearing." Patriots accused the Shakers of treason because they professed pacifism; and mainstream Christians branded them heretics, frequently interrupting the early meetings with violence and disturbing Shaker preaching missions and interviews. Mother Ann died while the little church still struggled to exist.

A revival movement in nearby New Lebanon, New York, provided a group of converts to the United Society; and they built a meetinghouse in New Lebanon in 1785 under the leadership of James Whittaker, designated the "Father" of the community even before Ann Lee's death. Father James' death, a year after Mother Ann's, resulted in the designation of Joseph Meacham, formerly a Baptist, as head of the Society.

Joseph Meacham, who soon selected and elevated Lucy Wright as head "in the female line," had himself been named "my Apostle in Ministry" by Mother Ann. Under the remarkable leadership of Meacham and Wright, missionaries were dispatched to Kentucky, to Ohio, and to anywhere else revivals were rumored to exist. The Shaker theology developed under their guidance, dance and song patterns emerged, and governmental structures grew.

Shaker life was communal, celibate, and celebrative. All incoming believers deeded their belongings to the community, accepted life in the family to which they were assigned, did the work as they were instructed, and pledged "Honest Industry" for the common good. Brothers and sisters shared equally in the leadership of each family (or group of ten to fifty adult believers). Likewise male and female Elders ruled each Shaker community, and formed the central ministry for the movement. Shakers gathered in each family for meals, lodging, division of labors, and sometimes for worship. As a community (or group of families in one location), most of the worship took place, as did the "union meetings," times of sheer conversation and sharing of feelings. However strict rules forbade unnecessary touching between the sexes, and even untoward or too frequent glances between a sister and a brother. Almost constant surveillance by family members assured adherence to these rules of conduct.

Shaker worship remained the cement of community life:

Come, come, Shaker life
Come life eternal
Come shake out of me
All that is carnal.

The Shakers gradually ritualized a variety of dances and song styles not uncommon among early nineteenth century Americans in general. In 1813 the songbook *Millenial Praises* standardized many heretofore wordless chants and solemn songs. A square-order shuffle, with straight ranks of men and women facing each other, remained popular. New worship "gifts" along the way included hand motions, introduced by Mother Lucy Wright in 1815, and ring dances, from 1822 onward. Spontaneous acts of stamping around an unbeliever, whirling, barking, and revelation reception became ceremonial adoptions in the worship itself. The "love gift," too, became evidently a medium of worship with brothers and sisters sometimes hugging and kissing one another (as the Bible bid them do). An address from an Elder usually came toward the end of the service, followed by another dance or song, or both.

The Shaker expectation of the world's impending cataclysm did not turn the believers from attending to the matters of this world. Symbolically, they hung chairs, candlestands, and other possible portables from pegboards each evening, so angel hosts would not be inhibited should they arrive during the night proclaiming the new creation. By the same token, wall-hung furniture made for efficient and thorough cleaning of the room. "Shaker your plate," a parental saying, came from the frugal habits of the Believers, and a host of Shaker poems and songs celebrated the virtues of believers, the vices of those outside.

Away with the sluggard, the glutton, and beast,
For none but the bee and the dove

Can truly partake of this heavenly feast
Which springs from the fountains of love.

Celibacy and rigidity in social constraints naturally limited Shaker growth. However Shaker salespeople traveled extensively, offering furniture, America's first flat-style brooms, quality herbs and seed, and various distinctive items from the score or more communities. They likewise preached Shakerism, directed prospective members to the communities, and accepted care of numerous orphaned children. At majority, children reared by the Shakers and educated in their schools, chose either to remain in the community or to join the outside world. These ways of recruiting believers yielded increases in Shaker communities through the 1830s when perhaps as many as five thousand followers of Mother Ann were active. Already a number of communities were in decline numerically during the 1850's, as millenial expectations began to decrease and modern society began its incredible impingement on the rurally-oriented enclaves. Spiritualism, conversations and experiences of communion with those already departed from the earth, had been a portion of early Shakerism; but its popularity increased during the middle decades of the movement. Gradually Shakerism became more of a curiosity among America's mainstream—less of a seemingly threat. Shakerism began a long and steady decline which would last throughout the century.

But the effects of Shakerism were considerable, upon both America's religious sects and mainstream communions as well. Both for social experimentation and religious commitment the Shakers deserve remembering and study.

The Rappites

The indefatigable traveler and careful observer of communes, Charles Nordhoff, visited Economy, Pennsylvania, in the early 1870s. He expressed his admiration for the remaining Harmonists but he felt sad that the promise of the experiment had in large measure passed away. "Once it was a busy place," he wrote, "for it had cotton, silk, and woolen factories, a brewery, and other industries." Even the hotel, formerly a delight for Pittsburgh visitors and travelers alike, no longer actively sought business. In spirit the Rappites had already ceased to be a vital community by the end of the Civil War.

The community began, and some think almost ended, with leadership from George Rapp (1759-1847). Born in Wurtemberg in a farming family, Rapp received a rudimentary education, and began work early in adolescence as a farmer and weaver. He soon married, and became in time the father of two children, John and Rosina. A good Christian and a student of the Bible, Rapp found himself regretting the disparity between the arid, rationalistic churches in the neighborhood, and the vital, caring community represented in the book of Acts. He shared his sentiments with others, and soon undertook preaching and holding worship services of a pietistic nature each Sunday. Although only a small group of like-minded people gathered to share with Rapp in worship, the clergy of the German Church found this activity a threatening one and resentfully imprisoned him for his "Separatism." Rapp was fined, but as a result of his notoriety and the warmth of his services more people came to join in. As Rapp's movement grew the threat of oppression did too. Finally he decided they should emigrate from Germany, and more than 300 families signaled their willingness to accompany him.

In 1804 the followers of Rapp established temporary communities in Pennsylvania and Maryland, and during the following year organized the "Harmony Society" in the river valley of the Connoquenessing. It was from the first a communistic enterprise, in which families lived as units but shared in the means and fruits of production. Increasingly the Rappites practiced various forms of asceticism as aids to reflection and piety. As a portion of the new discipline, Father Rapp and his wife undertook celibacy. John Rapp and his spouse followed suit. The viewed their commitment to celibacy as but a manner of preparing for the millenium and the perfect belief that would come. Gradually the "habit" of celibacy (for it was not law) became accepted for the most part as a "better way" for Christian life, a Pauline doctrine embodied.

John, along with some other members in the community, took exception to the habit, and quit the experiment. Secondary leadership passed to Rapp's adopted son, Frederick. The commune prospered in farming and distilling, however, and settled amicably with those withdrawing.

In 1814, the community moved to Indiana and bought 30,000 acres in the Wabash Valley. They built a whole town there, and more German immigrants augmented their numbers and skill bank. For the most part, Rappites were mechanics and crafts-people, accustomed to hard and fine work both in the shop and on the farm. Their care went into the construction of a church building also, described by William Hebert as "a noble church, the roof of which is supported in the interior by a great number of stately columns, which have been turned from trees of their own forest." The church structure was versatile, though, for it contained an upper storage compartment for storing grain and cotton, and a basement stocked with wine and cider. Like the Shakers, the Rappites mixed religious observance theologically with thoughtful, provident living.

Although the Indiana ground proved more bountiful than that of their former home, the Rappites found their personal energies sapped by malaria and their non-believing neighbors unpleasant. Therefore they sold their property to Robert Owen, and returned once again to Pennsylvania. This second time more precise in their selection of land to buy (they needed good grape-growing terrain), the Rappites settled to construct Economy. They did keep farming, but increasingly undertook manufacturing cloths and other durables for sale.

A number of Harmonists, wooed by a religious charlatan, Bernard Muller (alias Count Maximilian de Leon), left the commune in 1831. They took, as their portion of the assets, at least $105,000, with which they purchased some acreage not far from Economy. Their intention, to follow the Count's version of communal living (which permitted, encouraged, marriage), was clipped by the absconding of their new leader with most of the remaining funds from the settlement.

For his part, George Rapp exercised increasingly authoritarian powers as he grew older. The religious tenets which had arisen in rather free fashion became more rigid. In essence, the Rappites had always held beliefs in a dual Adam (before the fall "man" had contained both sexual elements), a dual Jesus (as second Adam, Jesus too embodied as God the maleness and femaleness of humanity), Christian communism, and believer baptism. Rapp, and his adopted son Frederick, wrote the community's hymns, led the worship, and managed the enterprise personally.

Hymns reflected the pietism and millenial hopes of the Rappites. They also provided vivid words of the community's images and symbols:

Harmony, your state of grace is here without fail,
Your rose-like beauty which by God Himself was made is
    reflected;
Through its fiery radiance God shines to earth.

***

Harmony, your magnificent splendor shall be honored
    at all times,
And your white dress of chastity, shows it righteousness;
So will chastity triumph and belong to God's friend
    who is closest to him,
And at the next meeting will present you like a king.

When George Rapp died, the community revised its code to provide for nine elders, two of whom would be trustees of the community. This pattern of leadership continued, with men only exercising formal control of affairs. Some documents, however, reflect the fact that Gertrude Rapp, granddaughter of George, held tacit authority in the governing of portion of the community. Life went on, but the thrust of the congregation's life seems to have been no longer toward the future so much as toward the past.

Mormon Migration

Among the developing communitarian movements and groups during the years of early nationalism, none stands out so forcefully as the Church of Jesus Christ of the Latter Day Saints. The Mormons have exercised an influence disproportionate to their numbers, which in 1860 were approximately 40,000. Like the Puritans of colonial America, they tried to meld all of life in a tightly-structured community—to encompass the religious and the secular life alike. And they usually remained, in those early years of the movement, unable or unwilling to differentiate the one from the other.

The Mormon Church was tied inseparably to its founder, Joseph Smith (1805-1844). Born in Vermont, Smith moved to Palmyra, New York, with his family in 1816. Western New York, in the years of Smith's adolescence, burned with revival fires of the mainstream and fringe churches alike. Periodically Smith's family converted to one or another of those churches. Young Joseph Smith later recalled times of intense religious experience which coincided with family decisions. One in particular Smith remembered. When in 1820 his family joined the Presbyterian Church, two angelic persons came to him and revealed that

> ...All religious denominations believing in incorrect doctrines, and that none of them was acknowledged of God as His Church and kingdom: and I was expressly commanded "to go not after them" at the same time receiving a promise that the fullness of the Gospel should at some future time be made known to me.

As such visions recurred, Smith finally received in 1827 certain "gold plates" and transcribed their ancient characters into English. He published in 1830 *The Book of Mormon*, a history of the migration of God's true church from Jerusalem to America. The work deals in extended fashion with social and theological questions of the day—How personal was God? What is the meaning of predestination? How theocratic should society be? How perfectable are people? What authority is there for the Christian gospel?

In the same year Smith started a church, a millenialist sect closely tied in stance to the contemporary communitarian experiments in nearby places (such as the one in Oneida) and to neighboring revivalist groups (such as the Campbellites). It was to be authoritarian in style, led by a priest-king "after the order of Melchizedek." Other Aaronic priests would lead the families, and all would work to guarantee religious vitality in the society.

When an increasing number of theologically articulate converts joined Smith, the sect flourished. Sidney Rigdon, an Ohio pastor and early convert, invited the group west. There self-educated Heber C. Kimball joined the sect and became an Apostle and a forceful Mormon missionary. Brother Heber journeyed as far as England to proclaim the power of the new church, but he remained for the most part in New York and New England channeling converts westward. Brigham Young joined the movement in the Spring of 1832, at about the same time Kimball did. Though Miriam, his wife, died that same fall, Young nevertheless led a Mormon party to Kirtland, Ohio, during the following July (1833). He spent considerable energies as a missionary, but he also assisted Smith in organizing the migration of the newly forming community to Jackson County, Missouri. Trouble, and armed anti-Smith raids from unsympathetic Missouri neighbors forced yet another Mormon move in 1838—to Commerce, Illinois, renamed "Nauvoo" by Joseph Smith.

Bolstered by the arrival of new converts, Mormons sought and received considerable authority from the State of Illinois. Again mutual aggravation and violence led to a Mormon exodus, but not before Joseph Smith and his brother Hyrum were murdered. They died at the hands of anti-Mormon rioters in the Carthage jail, where they had been incarcerated for "safekeeping" pending their own trial for rioting. Facts concerning the sequence of events are difficult to discover, but certainly the Church of the Latter Day Saints was undergoing a vitriolic split at the time. The *Nauvoo Expositor*, an anti-Smith press, was destroyed by Joseph and his party. Several sects split from the larger Mormon group at this time, one led by Joseph Smith, III, moved to Beloit, Wisconsin, and reorganized in 1852.

During February, 1846, initial Mormon units under the leadership of Young, Kimball, and other Apostles, began to cross hills and plains westward, with 12,000 Church members following during that year alone. Temporary settlements aimed finally at the Great Salt Lake region, and collaboration with the Polk administration's Mexican War efforts assisted the Mormons by providing them with some government funds for the move.

The authoritarian Church government organized itself likewise as a new State of Deseret administration. Young was the Governor, Kimball the Secretary of State, and another trusted leader, physician Willard Richards, Chief Justice. The Federal Government gave them no recognition as a state, however, and instead established only a Territory of Utah. Under President Fillmore, provisional governing authority was ceded to Young, at any rate.

America's nativism, rampant in its political Know-Nothingism during the 1850's, thrived on anti-Mormon accusations—they merely awaited the proper moment to declare their independence from the United States; they sanctioned polygamy (an open secret, confirmed as doctrine in 1852); they armed themselves to destroy unbelievers (called "Gentiles" by the Mormons). Hundreds of Mormons had migrated to Utah from other countries, as many as "seven out of ten" in the opinion of Democrat Stephen A. Douglas. True, too, were some assertions by residents of Utah from other religious bodies that Mormon "(in) justice" sided with Mormon litigants. By the same token, inferior federal officials assigned to the Utah territory frequently harassed the Latter Day Saints. In Washington executive and legislative ears—those of President Buchanan included—any allegation against the Mormon Church must have been true. A threatened Mormon "War" actually took place in 1857-1858, but it consisted mostly in a series of maneuvers by a federal force under Albert Sidney Johnston, and a parallel series of guerrilla actions by Lot Smith and other Mormon militia. The Mormon leaders sought and finally obtained their desired goal—a non-military accommodation with the government. The effected compromise, termed "Buchanan's Blunder" by Easterners frustrated in their anti-Mormon sentiments, was actually Brigham Young's triumph which signaled the beginning of Mormon acceptance in the U.S. It also signaled the beginning of the end of Mormonism as a self-conscious communitarian movement. The denomination, for it was one by now, settled down to building Mormon schools and churches, hospitals and missionary stations. The anti-Mormon nativists began to focus on the abolition of polygamy, the most radical doctrine of the sect still in effect. They succeeded in their lobby for the outlawing of polygamy in the U.S., and the first law against it passed in 1862.

Religious sentiments for and against the Saints moved from the arena of armed conflict into the American juridical system, where at least the differences in religious convictions could be settled without bloodshed, if they could not amicably be resolved. And the Mormons had moved in more than geographical terms, for they had by now accepted American racial, familial, and individualistic doctrines as a portion of their doctrine.

Brook Farm

Among the most famous, but least enduring communitarian efforts was the six year experiment called Brook Farm. Founded by George Ripley (1802-1880), and his wife Sophia, with considerable help from their friends, in the fall of 1841, The Brook Farm Institute of Agriculture and Education centered Boston's educational elite upon a utopian proving ground. The actual land, 170 acres of rather beautiful woods (and shallow topsoil), was purchased by a joint-stock company that included Charles A. Dana, later the publisher of the New York *Sun*, Nathaniel Hawthorne, Ripley's sister Marianne, and Minot Pratt, who, though inexperienced in farming, turned out to be an excellent agriculturalist. Pratt's family were mainstays of Brook Farm until almost the time of its dissolution. Other members came and stayed differing lengths of time. One of the most famous, Isaac T. Hecker, who subsequently founded the Paulist Society, proved among the best workers and bread bakers of the commune.

The core of owner-members was augmented by Transcendentalist, Unitarian, literary, artistic, and eccentric vistor-supporters, as well as by Ralph Waldo Emerson who was all of these and more. Margaret Fuller, writer of the Transcendentalist periodical the *Dial* and later critic for Greeley's *Tribune*, Orestes Brownson, who would become a major Catholic apologist, Bronson Alcott, the philosopher whose Fruitlands commune would build on the efforts of Brook Farm, and Elizabeth Peabody, a brilliant colleague of Emerson's, were frequently there and talking incessantly about the Farm with their audiences across the country. Theodore Parker, the young Unitarian minister in whose parish the Farm lay, would often stroll through West Roxbury on his way to and from the Farm. Many of the Brook Farmers attended Parker's Church, until he moved to Boston in 1845. Thus with so many people of skilled pen and voice, news of the commune spread widely, quickly.

Since Ripley himself had served as a Unitarian minister, one can argue that the Farm embodied the Unitarianism of the new generation. Indeed numbers of young men—Parker, William Henry Channing, nephew of William Ellery Channing and also a "man of the cloth," Emerson, and others— were ordained clergy. Morever, just as Unitarianism nurtured Transcendentalist thought so it also bred communitarian speculation: "How should people live together in harmony?"

"What is the relationship between humanity and nature, God, and personal growth?" "How shall innovative relationships be scientifically explored?" "What is transient in religion and economics? What is permanent?" Ripley, a prime instigator of the transcendentalist "Hedge Club" and a bright Harvard graduate (valedictorian, 1823) struggled with his wife and friends to answer these and other questions in life.

Brook Farmers turned the farmhouse into the Hive, the central community building, with sleeping rooms up and living areas downstairs. Laundry, nursery, and storage areas were added shortly. Another small house served as the school, until that portion of the commune's life was abandoned. In 1842, another house, the Eyrie, was constructed for the Ripleys and for several single members who had rooms there. Fourth and fifth dwellings were built by Mrs. A. G. Alford and Ichabod Morton who opened portions of these houses to the community. When Morton left after a very brief stay, his home the Pilgrim House, turned into a printery.

Not so radical in social design as the Shaker or Rappite communities, Brook Farm sported regular but cooperative family living with "free space" (board for work) for single persons. It was designed to profit from its school and its industries—farming, a commercial nursery, shoemaking, construction of sashes and blinds for houses, and others. Private maintenance of monies, mortgages on the properties, profits declared (although rarely), and pay for some members wanting "luxuries" all contributed toward making the commune a comparatively conservative place.

Theology and worship were indeed Unitarian, in that the ideals of "liberal Christianity" were guiding principles: worship should be in daily life; people should live in harmony with God, and with nature and other people; meaningless religious rituals should be brought to a screeching halt; and education would present the coming generation with progressive alternatives. Singing and playing music were religious activities, as were working and talking (especially talking).

Educationally, the preparatory school taught Latin, Italian, German, moral philosophy, English literature, Greek, mathematics, botany, history, music, and special classes could be arranged on practically any other subject. Brook Farmers thought they could gain in personal awareness, integrated education, by observing and participating in the reforms of the day. Thus though only the Ripleys and a few other members were actually members of the anti-slavery societies, whole wagon loads of them rode into Boston for debates and demonstrations.

In 1844, Albert Brisbane (1809-1890) convinced George Ripley, and probably Sophia also, that Fourierism was the social wave of the future. Brisbane had studied personally under Charles Fourier and was a thorough disciple the Frenchman's social science system. Ripley, too, came to believe that human nature does not change, and he already knew that industrialism was a curse on the human race. Brisbane spent increasing time at Brook Farm arguing the merits of Fourierism, with its emphasis on work by differing groups in diversified tasks, communal living in a human phalanx, and justice in the social system. Brisbane's *Social Destiny of Man* (1840) represented an outline of "Attractive Industry, Human Harmony," and other nice sounding ideas. With a number of dissenters and a few participants withdrawing, the Brook Farmers decided to undertake living in the style of Fourier. They proceeded to build a "phalanstery," the first requisite of the orthodoxy.

Fourierism never really had a chance for success in Brook Farm, for the almost completed phalanstery burned. The members of the commune began to desert Ripley, leaving him with a heavy personal debt he eventually paid. Though its ending seems very sad, Brook Farm gave to Americans a promise of alternative living possibilities within the capitalist system. It likewise buttressed the growing process of perhaps the finest generation of American scholars ever. Its ideas and mistakes led also to the comparative success of yet another experiment—Oneida.

The Oneida Community

Established by John Humphrey Noyes (1811-1886), the Oneida Community followed perfectionist theology, radical patterns of familial life, and progressive economics. Thus its story is both the biography of its founder and a recitation of its accomplishments and experiments. It came as a "second generation" community, intentionally seeking to avoid the pitfalls discovered in Shakerism and especially in Brook Farm.

Noyes himself was born in 1811, in a well-to-do family. He attended Dartmouth College and Andover Seminary before Yale Divinity School, where Nathaniel Taylor preached revival and human potential with such telling effects. Noyes was convicted and convinced, declared his belief in the accomplishment of the *parousia*, the Second Coming of Christ, and committed himself to Christian perfection as preparation of the dawning eschaton. Refused ordination because of his heterodoxy, Noyes undertook preaching anyhow and leading a little group of appreciative persons in the theology of Christian perfection. He published with another man, James Boyle, a paper called *The Perfectionist*. Integral to Noyes' theology, both during and following the association with Boyle, was a reinterpretation of the meaning of marriage. The institution, as Noyes' viewed it in nineteenth century America, was full of "exclusiveness, jealousy, quarrelling," and a sign of human "apostasy" from God's design.

When Noyes himself "married," he contracted with his wife-to-be (and disciple in perfectionism) Harriet Holton to allow no limit in "the range of our affections." The Noyes' had five children, four of whom were stillborn. Around John and Harriet Noyes in Putney, Vermont, gathered John's sisters Harriet and Charlotte, a brother George, and some other persons. A Society of Inquiry was organized in 1841, the first communal experiment based on Noyes' theology. This was the central gathering of such believers, but not the only one, as Noyesians began similar societies in Brooklyn, and elsewhere. With the pooling of group resources, especially money, a Putney Corporation was created to handle the purse.

Evidently while still in Putney the communitarians began to practice "Complex Marriage," a vital doctrine of this perfectionism which called for male continence in *coitus reservatus* and the possibility of all males becoming spouses of all females within the Society. Noyes taught that Complex Marriage was an eschatological institution, a social evidence of the dawning millenium.

Rumors of the "free love" and "communism" in the Putney Society of Inquiry brought threats to members of the commune in 1847. Noyes was imprisoned and charged with "adultery." Upon release, he received counsel of some disciples and dispersed the group to reconstitute the commune at the home of Jonathan Burt, near Oneida, New York. Burt had been converted by Noyes and had undertaken to establish a satellite Society there some months previous to the trouble in Putney.

At Oneida a Mansion House was the first building constructed for the whole commune. As described in an official report, the House built was "sixty-feet long, thirty-five feet wide, three stories high and ...surmounted by a cupola." The first floor contained kitchen, dining room, and cellar; the second, a parlor, reception-room, school-room, and printery; the third, sleeping apartments for couples and for single women; and the garret, a dormitory for single men. Another building, a part of the old farm and sawmill, became the nursery for care of young children.

Noyes remained the charismatic leader, and other early participants were known as "Central Members." They professed to live a true "Christian communism," the way of life described in Acts. At first they sought to live primarily by farming, but soon they turned back to trades they knew and occupations that made more money. They maintained the sawmill, set up a blacksmith shop, and initiated the manufacture of animal traps. In time that item would prove perhaps their most marketable product, although the volume sold varied drastically from year to year. They had not yet begun the sale of silk thread or silver-plate by the time of the Civil War, but already in 1863 proceeds that they described as "profit" from various enterprises amounted to $44,755 as their annual report indicated. Gradually the number of members increased also through the decade of the 1850's, almost all from new conversions and joinings rather than from additions of children. They had not yet begun the practice of *stirpiculture* (race-improvement) which would characterize their latter years.

Both sexes evidently shared housework and waiting on tables, although in their custom of employing skills with which people came to the community, more men usually worked as mechanics and ironmongers as most of the women did the sewing and knitting. Frequently "bees"—apple paring, gathering cowslips, shelling peas, and the like—were run to break the monotony of routine work. Even the most skilled persons apparently switched jobs from time to time with others less skilled in a craft in order to keep a sense of participation vibrant among all the members in all the activities.

The Oneida community, and its companion group in Wallingford, Connecticut, practiced the ordinance of criticism, introduced by Noyes as a mix of group discussion and personal improvement. He recalled the efficacy of this practice at Andover seminary, in a group he communed with there. Participants, who were supposed to be open to growth possibilities in both spirit and mind, offered themselves for criticism. The members would talk and the person being criticized would receive their remarks in silence. As Oneida grew in numbers, a Club was appointed to carry out most of the criticism, but occasionally all would still gather in the Mansion House to engage in it. At least a portion of the inter-change, historical criticism, sounds like a kind of psycho-therapy. In Noyes' words, "the result has been numerous confessions of wrongs in the past that had lain secret—per-haps half forgotten—but necessarily darkening and poison-ous to present experience."

The "faith-cure" was also a portion of the life, worship, and ethics of the community. Members occasionally "cast out evil spirits" that caused disease; and when a contagion struck the community, (whooping cough, for instance) they might hold a "Meeting of Indignation" to protest the exis-tence of some demonic incursion into their perfection. They considered all life to be a fabric, and paid great attention to the food ingested as source of health or illness. This care about "alimentiveness," as they called it, extended to include the balancing of differing foods and portions of foods. Prayer evidently remained a major ingredient in Oneida life, and it was viewed as a part of the daily regimen for all.

Just as work, eating, sex, and "ordinances" were thought-fully considered, so the Oneidans consciously decided about appropriate recreation. Early in their community, marching was a vital portion of their spare-time life. Occasionally they would continue to form ranks and to march, a symbol of their concerted efforts. They also took to dancing, although the "outside" world of culture frequently deprecated such activity. They formed a community orchestra, and they put on dramas and improvisations. Segregated by sexes, they also took turns at swimming.

In short, life seemed comparatively full in the community, and Noyes meant to be flexible to accommodate some changes as time went by. Perhaps this mix of work and radical living, of piety and "perfection," was disappointing in the long run for the commune did not succeed in establishing others in its image (with the exception of Wallingford, whose members were almost interchangeable with the Oneidans). Whatever the feelings of members over the years, it remained a vital human community during the years under consideration—a major landmark in the utopian efforts of Americans.

5

American Theologians

Many of the issues basic to American theology and ethics during the period had already been mentioned—the grappling with particularism and inclusivism in the nation's free church environment, the relationship between revelation and scriptural authority, the struggle to discern meaning of "religious community" and "religious life," and for Christians specifically the reconciling of Calvinist and Arminian views of the nature of human existence and salvation. But the differing communions, as they remained introspective, offered overwhelming variety in the articulated alternatives and possible directions presented. Thus it may be helpful to sojourn in some detail with a few of the theologians who fashioned religious thought in that era, and to outline their respective positions regarding the questions of the day.

Three theologians—Charles Hodge, Horace Bushnell, and Theodore Parker—become for us "case studies" in the practice of articulating theology in the first half of the nineteenth century. All three drew on the main tradition of Puritanism, and all represented segments of the American population for which they spoke. In addition, all three set the pattern for a subsequent heritage though the followers of each varied immensely in the extent to which they "conserved" the thought of their mentors.

Charles Hodge, the conservative, began his career and

remained at Princeton Seminary for almost all his life. In his teaching and writing, his arguments and leadership of the Presbyterians, Hodge represented the continuity of nineteenth century Calvinism with its progenitors.

Horace Bushnell, whose mediational theology managed both to preserve portions of Calvinism and yet to begin a liberal educational tradition in mainstream American religion, occupied a thoroughly middle territory in the spectrum of the theologians. He brought to bear new ways of thinking about Christian language, nurture, and the work of Christ. At the same time, he sought reform in very limited fashion, and he relied in large measure on the reinterpretation of traditional categories of theology.

Theodore Parker provided a revolutionary ministry, both in the religious life he led and in the theology he articulated. Parker tried to bridge all the gaps of his day between science and religion, Christianity and other religions, and societal patterns and ethical hopes.

Charles Hodge (1797-1878)

From its roots to its leaves, the theology of Charles Hodge was conservative. That he piously and stolidly lived the theology he professed was a rather universal observation by others of the man personally. "A symbol of orthodoxy," a white bone walking-stick passed to Hodge by his mentor in the Princeton theology, Archibald Alexander, was dutifully passed along by Charles to his son A.A. Hodge—unchanged. In almost an equally unmitigated state, the theology of American Calvinism received by Hodge was that transmitted to the thousands of persons studying with him through the years. It represented Calvinist "orthodoxy" not only for the period now studied, but for the remainder of the nineteenth century as well.

Born in Philadelphia, Hodge grew to adolescence carefully nurtured in a Christian family. His mother, Mary Blanshard, came from a formerly Huguenot family, and Charles' father

Hugh, who died when the son was still an infant, boasted Scotch-Irish stock. The young man attended Princeton both for undergraduate studies and for theological seminary. Graduated in 1819, he soon was appointed to the faculty of the seminary. There he remained until his death, except for brief interludes of study and teaching elsewhere.

Hodge arranged to study in Germany and Switzerland during an early sabbatical in 1826-1828, where his exposure to the innovative theologies of Friedrich Schleiermacher and others simply confirmed him in orthodoxy. He returned convinced of the essential changelessness of Christian truth, not to mention the immutibility of God. In the words of J.O. Nelson, "By mid-century, Hodge's own attitude had been generally recognized as the characteristic expression of the Princeton theology in its classic form."

Hodge gave his time to writing and to churchmanship, as well as to study and teaching. As editor of *The Biblical Repertory* and *The Princeton Review*, Hodge furthered his presentation of essential Calvinism throughout America. He likewise wrote commentaries on the Books of *Romans* (1835), *Corinthians* (1857, 1859), and *Ephesians* (1860). His study of *The Constitutional History of the Presbyterian Church in the United States of America* emphasized the confessional bases of the communion and the proper actions of the Old School party. And Hodge's mammoth *Systematic Theology* (3 volumes, 1872-1873) gave polished form to the doctrines he had taught and lived for decades.

Christian piety, Hodge insisted, lay at the very center of the faith. He himself had been reared in the "covenant," and so most members of the church seemed to be. In "doing theology," he was simply putting into words the faith that he had received implicity in the Christian community. Hodge recognized, however, that not all persons grew to maturity in such a grace-full environment, and he sought to affect the lives of those around him as he preached and evangelized according to the biblical understanding of the gospel. In like manner, Hodge considered that Calvin preached piety as focal in Christian commitment, and that evangelism was a Christian duty for all Presbyterians. Yet he scorned what seemed the false piety and hollow evangelism of the revivalists, who depended not on the covenant but rather on technique for a "conversion."

Scripture was the authoritative way for Christians to discern God's manner and acts of salvation. It surpassed all human understanding, and it was "folly" to those who did not participate in the covenant of grace. To those who lived in Christ, though, Scripture self-evidently proclaimed God's special relationship with believers. Hodge declared, in a popular work for the American Sunday School Union, *The Way of Life*, that the Bible's authority

> consists mainly in its perfect holiness in correspondence between all its statements respecting God, man, redemption, and a future state, and all our own right judgments, reasonable apprehensions, and personal experiences.

The Bible, in sum, was the "rule of faith and practice," as the Westminster Standards proclaimed. It had been inspired by God in full (plenary inspiration) and was revealed for Christians of all ages. Jesus Christ himself had testified to the essential authority of the Bible. In addition, the "facts" of the Bible are self-authenticating and need no outside community to put a stamp of approval on them. By the scientific method, inductively, we know the Bible to present truth. In this logic, as elsewhere, Hodge traded on the philosophy of the school of Scotch Realism popular at the time.

Hodge emphasized God's sovereignty, the traditional Trinitarian expressions of it in the creeds, and the Westminster lists of God's attributes that illuminated it. The Calvinistic distinction between "ordained power" and "absolute power," a divine possibility of intervening to overrule secondary causes, Hodge maintained as important to comprehending the manner in which the world operates. For

Hodge, God was forever "Just." Justice did not find merely a wrathful expression as God related to the world, although from time to time God's actions could indeed appear too wrathful. Moreover, the Bible does sometimes describe God as wrathful. But primarily in Scripture and in life, God's justice was loving, holy, and wise.

God's decrees, basic ingredients in the Westminster Standards, Hodge did not neglect. He usually refrained from long expositions on the subject of "double predestination," however, content to let the matter be addressed by other people. Generally Hodge accepted an infralapsarian interpretation of election, assuming predestination and election to have occurred within time rather than that before all creation such decisions were inexorable in the design of God.

Whatever his reluctance to speak of election to reprobation, Hodge did not feel any compunction about discussing human depravity. Original sin, imputed to Adam and to all the race from Adam's sin, Hodge considered a universal "fact." That was the starting point for human beings one and all—the universal condition—that sin was a condition of their lives. Sinful humanity both failed to do the law, and did what is contrary to the law. Hodge sometimes excepted infants from this blanket condemnation, but he included all self-aware persons as in the category of "the justifiably guilty."

In this situation the work of Christ was for justification of those ordained to life. As he talked of the nature of Christ, Hodge remained carefully Chalcedonian—he desired to affirm the full humanity of Jesus Christ as well as his full divinity. Concerning the work of Christ, Hodge spoke in forensic terms, using the language of courts and laws. Christ accomplished "satisfaction" and received in his death the penalty which would justifiably be exacted from sinful humanity. The atonement, or work of reconciliation of people with God for their salvation, Hodge considered a limited affair. Thus for the elect to justification God's grace through Christ makes grace for human response. Righteousness is imputed, as sin was imputed, through the covenant of grace and the work of Christ. Gradually the Christian proceeds in a pattern of growth in Christ—sanctification—to be completed only in glory.

The Church, or covenant community, is both visible and invisible, as Saint Augustine (then Calvin) perceived it. Hodge treated both visible and invisible Churches. The true Church, composed of saints, was known only to God but not totally unrelated to the earthly Church. The saints experienced community with each other and communion with God, the work of the Holy Spirit, and gradual sanctification. Gradually and inexorably, God also calls for profession of faith by Christians and the organization of congregations and judicatories in society. The work of the Church in the world serves to discipline the saints in their piety. The visible Church, though sometimes in error (by changing) seeks proper relations with the State, care of the poor, publication of the Word, a context for real worship, etc. Reforms were necessary in the world, for Hodge, as long as they conformed society to Biblical admonitions. Thus he struggled for Sabbath observance especially, and against Sunday train service, mail delivery, and the opening of stores. He also favored the reform efforts of the American Sunday School Union, which sold 35,000 or more copies of *The Way of Life* for him. Since slavery was scriptural, therefore slaveowners did not sin any more than other people. And since women's rights had been outlawed by Paul, Hodge would broach no reform there either. Thus he remained consistently siding with the Southern elements in Old School Presbyterianism, and sought their continuation of the Assembly even after hostilities broke out between North and South in the War.

The whole Christian enterprise (more properly, in Hodge's mind "God's whole enterprise for Christians") was supernatural. Thus Hodge was extremely interested in, but critical of, Horace Bushnell's theology of nurture as it appeared.

Hodge wrote a review of *Christian Nurture* which appeared in *The Princeton Review* (1847), accusing Bushnell of propounding "a naturalistic doctrine concerning conversion." He could not help but notice how Bushnell accentuated the family influence, as his personal experience verified. But he lamented Bushnell's conclusions, as well as the latter's reform efforts.

Seldom treated seriously by scholars because he expressed a theology so thoroughly "borrowed," Charles Hodge may well have influenced nineteenth century theology the most of any one American. His students were from all evangelical traditions, not just Presbyterian, and his conservatism lasted another two or three uninterrupted generations as many of them followed Hodge's direction.

Horace Bushnell (1802-1876)

Scholars have described Horace Bushnell with accuracy as a "transitional figure" who introduced new theological horizons not only in thinking about Christian nurture, but in understanding Christology, soteriology (doctrine of salvation), and ecclesiology (doctrine about the Church) as well. He, as Charles Hodge, "forever" located in one place for ministry. Bushnell served continually as pastor of the North Church (Congregational) of Hartford, Connecticut, from 1833 until bad health forced his retirement in 1861. But his thought and influence ranged broadly and affected a growing "middle ground" among American Christians.

Born of a farming family, Bushnell attended schools and the Congregational church near his home in New Preston, Connecticut. He graduated from Yale in 1826 and taught school, staffed a commercial journal, studied law, and served as a Yale tutor before a religious experience convinced him to develop his faith and to serve in ministry. He studied at Yale Divinity School, profoundly influenced by Nathaniel Taylor's preaching and leadership, as well as by Samuel Taylor Coleridge's *Aids to Reflection*.

Bushnell was ordained to ministry in Hartford's North Church in May, 1833, and married Mary Apthorp of New Haven that fall. He sought in his ministry to avoid the party strife that arose between Old School and New School theologians, to preserve a comprehensive Christianity encompassing both points of view.

Bushnell's popularity, and the beginnings of notoriety as well, came with the publication of *Christian Nurture* in 1847. There his assertion, "that the child is to grow up a Christian, and never know himself as being otherwise," began to describe and outline a program for religious education of children. He meant his work to supplement those of other people who concentrated on religious conversion experiences. It is not that Bushnell deprecated revivals at this time, after all he personally remembered meaningful times of such intensity as others described. Rather Bushnell recognized the organic nature of the family, and he sought to harness this relationship to encourage discipline of children in the faith. The church practice of baptizing infants had long relied on this knowledge, though only tacitly. "The very command, 'believe and be baptized,' of which so much is made, is exactly met...for the child, being included as it were in the parental life, is accounted presumptively one with the parents and sealed with the seal of their faith."

Bushnell emphasized such particulars as family prayers, family government, a child's stages in personal development, and the creative use of holidays and Sundays in order to lead the child in Christian growth. "Religion, being the supreme end and law of life," he contended; "is to have everything put in the largest harmony with it."

Bushnell argued that Christian nurture was the solemn duty of all parents—that Christians had the obligation to "outstock" the irreligious and heathen peoples of the world and so to populate the world with believers for the coming kingdom. He claimed this responsibility for all Christians, but he described it particularly for those in the Reformed tradition. He, and others in that heritage, relied on covenant theology, and a doctrine of predestination, for spiritual sustinence. Those people especially who believed in covenants knew that parenting was a sacred trust for positive effects. Adults could not think it the responsibility of God to call and convert people grown up without heuristic models of Christian discipleship. While God could accomplish anything desired by miraculous means, miracles of lasting conversions were rare in fact; and Christian piety normally springs from those with committed parents and grandparents. The work of Christ, and that of the Holy Spirit, as the Bible portrays it, comes in concert with human commitment to foster piety among people:

> A camp meeting, or a band of pilgrims gathered for a single week, a thousand miles from home, may well enough desire such kind of preaching as will serve the zest of the occasion. But it is no design of Christianity to get by the need of intelligence, and fashion a sanctity that has no fellowship with dignity. A regularly instituted Christian congregation, who are to live and grow up on the same spot, from age to age, it has long ago been discovered, must be compelled to gird up the loins of the mind.

It was the family, both genetically and congregationally that built up a person in spiritual wisdom. Therein the work of God flourished most surely.

If Calvinists such as Hodge had questions about the supernaturalism of Bushnell's theology of nurture and its orthodoxy, they were confirmed in doubting his conformity by Bushnell's subsequent effort—*God in Christ* (1849). Bushnell himself declared that his religious source was in part another experience—a direct revelation. Reviews of the work excoriated this Calvinist-heretic, and brought Bushnell personal isolation from former colleagues in the ministerial consociation.

The work offered sections on "Divinity of Christ," "The

Atonement," and on "Dogma and Spirit." Actually each essay had been delivered at a school of divinity (Yale, Harvard, and Andover, respectively). There was some reinterpretation of orthodoxy in each. Bushnell said that Jesus Christ was not properly understood in either the exclusive claims of the Unitarians or those of the Trinitarians. It was the part about the Trinitarians that drew ire:

> This theory of two distinct subsistencies, still maintaining their several kinds of action in Christ,—one growing learning, obeying, suffering; the other infinite and impassible—only creates difficulties a hundred fold greater than it solves. It virtually denies any real unity between the human and the divine, and substitutes collocation or copartnership for unity.

In place of this confusion, Bushnell modestly offered a reassessment of the Christian tradition that regarded the nature of Christ as a mystery, unfathomable, and worthy of meditation beyond words. "God is, in the most perfect and rigid sense, one being—a pure intelligence, undivided, indivisible, and infinite," he said, with a following qualification: "Whatever may be true of the Father, Son, and Holy Ghost, it certainly is not true that they are three distinct consciousnesses, wills, and understandings." Rather eternally they worked ("it worked") instrumentally as three.

The atonement, Bushnell contended, had been misrepresented in purely penal language. He wished to focus discussion and theories primarily on the "speculative and ritual" forms of an authentic doctrine, an occurence in both subjective and objective reality. Thirdly, Bushnell argued that ecclesiastical formulations of dogma long crystalized were entirely too important to the churches. Resulting from their dependence on dogma, over organic doctrine, was the present condition of church fragmentation. Instead Bushnell proposed Christian unity:

> One thing is clear, that the highest form of piety can never appear on earth until the disciples of Christ are

able to be in the Spirit, in some broader and more permanent sense than simply to suffer those local and casual fervors that may be kindled within the walls of a church, or the boundaries of a village. The Spirit of God is a catholic spirit, and there needs to be a grand catholic reviving, a universal movement, penetrating gradually and quickening into power the whole church of Christ on earth.

Most interesting of all Bushnell's assertions in *God in Christ*, however, was his prefatory treatise on language. Bushnell described the power of visual images summoned by words, and the power of language itself. He recalled the meaning and wisdom of religious vocabulary particularly, but he dismissed any possibility of certain formulations having a power to "save" people. Imprecision lies at the very form of words, he stated, as well as in their meaning. In addition, communication of ideas through words, much less religious insight and revelation, cannot but fail when done in language by human beings. It can never be a perfect transmission of any idea or revelation, although it can be trusted as a process within the limits of human endeavor. Thus confidence in dogma was not only "mitigated" in Bushnell's day, it should be mitigated.

After the writing of *God in Christ*, Bushnell continued to publish his theology, and to minister in Hartford, despite opposition. He sought an end to slavery, though he did not belong to violent abolitionist groups. Later, and regrettably, he produced works deprecating the potential for black America to contribute anything substantial to culture, and he likewise ridiculed the suffragist movement as a "reform against nature." But he represented in these attitudes the opinions of mid-America of the day, and reflected the myopia of his humanity. In his theological categories, Bushnell approached both the conservatism of Hodge at times and the radical Unitarianism of Parker, an acquaintance of Bushnell if not a close friend.

Theodore Parker

The theology of Theodore Parker was truly a "high-water mark" in the thought of the era. Radical in its implications for Christian living, it offered both a thoroughgoing hope in the future of the nation and world and a reliance on the pervasive religious tradition that informed American society. Nevermind that its optimism proved naive, and its precept largely unheeded, Parker's system did offer a viable liberal alternative to the prevalent orthodoxy of ante-bellum America.

Born in Lexington, Massachusetts, in 1810, Parker attended Harvard and graduated from the Divinity School. He was invited to attend, and began at once to participate, in the "Hedge Club" or inner circle of Transcendentalists, because of his interest and his intellectual acumen. He remained a minister and pastor, first at West Roxbury's Spring Street Congregation (near Book Farm) and then in the Twenty-Eighth Street Congregation in Boston, organized for him by laypeople who sought his leadership.

Parker was a pastor-reformer, preaching and writing, speaking and fund-raising in behalf of myriad progressive goals—disinvolvement in military imperialism, public education, women's rights, penal reform, a medical treatment of mental imbalance, labor rights, temperance, and realignment of the means of production from crude capitalism to a kind of democratic socialism. Primarily, though, he sought abolition of slavery from American society. No Disunionist, even though he moved in the first rank of Garrisonian thinkers, Parker considered that as fellow Americans, Northerners had the obligation to rid the south of its peculiar institution. He conspired to overthrow every attempt to enforce the Fugitive Slave Law of 1850. His "Vigilance Committee" actively fought each governmental action to return an escaped slave, and Parker himself was once arrested and tried for "inciting to riot" the people of Boston in this effort. An ardent supporter of John Brown in Kansas, Parker both encouraged

Brown to precipitate a slave insurrection in the south and then defended the man publicly after events at Harper's Ferry.

Parker's theology invited such forceful behavior. He worked to distinguish the "popular theology" from the revolutionary effects of "Primitive Christianity." In one characteristic sermon, "Primitive Christianity," preached at John Sargent's Suffolk Street Chapel in Boston, December 26, 1841, he summarized its nature: primitive Christianity changed John, James, Peter and the rest of the men and women in the early church from defeated members of the human race into thoroughgoing revolutionaries. Paul especially, who in Parker's opinion seriously misunderstood the "gospel" and who needlessly complicated the faith, nevertheless evidenced "a striking instance of the power of real Christianity to recast the character" of those persons it infected. "It is not marvelous," Parker reasoned, "these men were reckoned unsafe persons. Nothing in the world is so dangerous and untractable as one who loves man and God." Love of God and other people were, according to Parker, "the weapons with which to pluck the oppressor down from his throne."

Parker knew God as easy to love, the "Perfect Divine Parent." Throughout his ministry, Parker based his "Absolute Religion" on this theological cornerstone. As he looked back, Parker remembered:

> I have taught that God contains all possible and conceivable perfection:—the perfection of being, self-subsistence, conditioned only by itself; the perfection of power, all-mightiness; of mind, all-knowingness; of conscience, all-righteousness; of affection, all-lovingness; and the perfection of that innermost element, which in finite man is personality, all-holiness, faithfulness to Himself.

God was also Divine. Though he seldom resorted to the use of such an apparent tautology, Parker did imply both that the "popular religion" taught the obverse of God's divinity and that he accentuated properly God's deity. By instructing believers that God's will changed when one prayed, the churches sacrificed truth about God's divinity in order to maintain antiquated institutions. In contrast, he stated that "The idea of God as the infinite may exhaust the most transendent imagination."

Perfection and Divinity were linked with Parenthood; and God was thus Parent for Parker, no longer merely "Father." Although he did resort to the name "Father" for God on occasion, Parker carefully designated God as "Parent" whenever he consciously considered the matter. In doing this, Parker emphasized that God's actions often appear to us more closely associated with motherhood than with fatherhood. He wanted "to express more sensibly the quality of tender and unselfish love," and he believed parenthood carried that meaning.

If God was infinite and perfect, people (humankind) could be perfectible. Each person began life an innocent "Adam," "just as new and fresh, just as near to God as the first father and mother." Human beings were not "worms," as Parker characterized orthodox theologians to pretend they were. Rather they were meant to become "men" (for generic use of that word still had currency). This "manhood" could be for everyone, and the idea that some few alone had been chosen for perfection in immortality became for Parker a ridiculous misunderstanding of the possibilities and a misrepresentation of God's intentions for humanity.

Jesus, by the same token, was not merely "the pipe on which God plays," but rather introduced all people to a new horizon in "humanhood." "There was manly intellect joined with womanly conscience and affection and soul," he declared. The natural corollary—that followers of Jesus need of all people be the most free—was Parker's focus in understanding the nature of the church. It should become a "society for the promotion of the truth." All life properly would be encompassed in church life, and *vice versa*, so that people would live the sacramental existence God called them to.

In cooperating with God in gradual perfection of the universe and of themselves, people naturally would be progressive. Progress, while continual (that is, recurrent) was not necessarily continuous or uninterrupted. Human beings could either impede the natural processes or cooperate with them. Herein lay the real miracle of existence. Parker emphasized throughout the pervasive, miraculous operation of natural law. "Compared to the wonders of law, the tales of miracles of the Old Testament and the New, are no fact, but poor poetry." he decided. "They are like ghosts among a market full of busy men...."

Speaking of the Old and New Testaments, Parker might be imagined to have deprecated the Scriptures with such a natural theology. However, quite the contrary, he took great interest in them, read them devotionally, and sought to memorize all the passages he could. One of his first works, a translation with notes of Wilhelm DeWette's *Introduction to the Old Testament*, made available to English readers the heretofore limited knowledge of biblical criticism from German scholarship so important to Moses Stuart and others.

In spite of all his ideas and interests, Parker remained a theologian-minister. He claimed to be the "Minister-at-Large," to undertake the "socialization of Christianity."

> The minister aims to be, to do, and to suffer, in special for his own particular parish, but also and in general for mankind at large. He proposes for himself this end, the elevation of mankind,—their physical elevation to health, comfort, abundance, skill, and beauty; their intellectual elevation to thought, refinement, and wisdom; their moral and religious elevation to goodness and piety, till they all become as sons of God also, and prophets. However his direct and main business is to

promote the spiritual growth of men, helping them to love one another, and to love God.

His pulpit Parker viewed as a "place to stand and move the world." Pastoral visits he saw as opportunities to influence people "in joy and grief," as weddings and funerals provided contact with persons who were either "flushed with hope" or "wrung with pain." In other words, Parker extrapolated his doctrine to meet life situations which he encountered. The theology demanded four ideals for which he sought to strive—democracy, freedom for everyone, equality of opportunity, and human welfare were guiding goals in which other specific projects and goals made sense.

Thus Parker differed with the "Know-Nothings" and considered their anti-Catholicism wrong. He declined to join them with the memorable disclaimer that he "should prefer a higher law Catholic to a lower law Protestant." "Democracy must rest on humanity, not mere nationality or on modes of religion," he maintained. By the same logic, Parker invited suffragists to his home, where he and his wife Lydia Cabot solidified the movement in organization. He found "the woman question," as reformers of the day termed it, inextricable from political and ecclesiastical reform. He posited that "woman is to correct man's taste, mend his morals, excite his affections, inspire his religious faculties." All that sounded rather condescending; but he continued to speculate that if women were in government, the enfranchisement of the poor and gains in public education would indubitably result. Education of women would aid the cause of abolition, and the amelioration of the working class would occur if women received their rightful place of equality in management. Like theology and life, the reforms were all a fabric of interwoven strands.

A coterie of "Parkerites" sought to carry on the theology of Theodore after his death in 1860, but they went in numbers of different directions. O.B. Frothingham and Moncure D. Conway carried on the tradition in Unitarianism for awhile, and Thomas Wentworth Higginson and F.B. Sanborn moved into the fields of literature and social science respectively. The theology was brought into Unitarianism, and more particularly into the Free Religious Association that split to its left. And portions of Parker's thought and activity made inroads into the American mainstream in subsequent decades.

6

The Impulse for Reform

Emerson declared grandiloquently that anybody in New England should be struck in 1844 with how enormous reform activity had become. "His attention must be commanded by the signs that the Church, or religious party, is falling from the church nominal, and is appearing in temperance and non-resistance societies, in movements of abolitionists and of socialists, and in very significant assemblies, called Sabbath and Bible Conventions—composed of ultraists, of seekers, of all the soul of the soldiery of dissent, and meeting to call into question the authority of the Sabbath, of priesthood, and of the church." Emerson's sentence, a mouthful indeed if he spoke it in one breath, seemed to grasp a number of salient features of the reform movements during the period. He pronounced both on the religious basis of the reforms and also on the commitment of the persons seeking change. It was in large measure the "devout" people who led reforms, although they differed greatly on the object and means of devotion. And they were in every way sincere, not playing reform as some later historians have intimated.

Emerson caught also the irony of the reform movements, that frequently they worked against each other. A serious split developed between workers for abolition and those who sought anti-slavery along with women's rights. The American Tract Society produced numbers of pamphlets which supported the continuance of slavery. The denominatinal benevolent societies often competed with the ecumenical groups devoted to the same ends. And the nativist societies and parties constricted freedom even as other reform groups sought to bring freedom to people not yet enjoying it.

However complicated they are to discuss, reforms were part and parcel of the ante-bellum religious experience. There were the specifically evangelical reform movements—the American Tract Society, seeking to distribute Christian apologetics for evangelism and education, the American Bible Society, printing the Scripture in bulk "without note or comment," and the American Sunday School Union, so near to the heart of Charles Hodge. There were social reforms— the American Peace Society, active especially at the time of the Mexican War, the American Education Society, geared toward establishing a public ability to read all the tracts and Bibles being produced, and the American Colonization Society, seeking manumission of black people but also their remission to Africa. There were also the reforms not so easily categorized—the American Party, for instance, which idolized mainstream Protestantism to the detriment of Christianity, yet operated with many of the same leaders as the other movements. Societies also existed to stop Sunday mail delivery (which accomplished their goal), to insure full Sabbath observance, to reduce drunkenness, to save "fallen" women, to send missionaries both "domestic" and "foreign," and to reduce brutality in prisons, reformatories, and asylums. On and on goes the list of benevolent enterprises, many of which still exist in some form or other.

Three of the reforms stand out today as perhaps the most influential upon American life—the quests for temperance, women's rights, and anti-slavery. Constricted space prohibits discussion of all but these movements. Temperance began as a crusade alongside the rise of Methodism. Most of the directions of the reform were already undertaken by the time of the Civil War, although the Prohibition Amendment still was decades away. The movement for women's rights had barely begun by mid-century, and by way of contrast to temperance throngs, only a small portion of the reformers had embraced it. Anti-slavery, by all accounts the most pervasive of the impingements on American life during the nineteenth century, yielded at once the greatest reforming fervor and the largest "backlash." Exploration of these three reforms, however, can give a glimpse into the whole spectrum.

Temperance and Prohibition

Most Methodists, taking their cues from John Wesley and his American Bishop Asbury, perceived that alcoholic beverages were inherently evil. They were not alone in this view since many Quakers also affirmed abstinence from hard liquor as a desirable way of life. In addition, Dr. Benjamin Rush of Philadelphia produced in 1784 his *Inquiry into the Effect of Ardent Spirits on the Human Body and Mind*. Rush praised the comparative safety of opium over alcohol as a "less addictive" medicine, and he advocated total abstinence from the latter. Rush, and the Methodists too, linked the use of alcohol with the committing of crime, the loss of dignity, and the general deterioration of the society. Rush himself began speaking against the "liquor traffic," and in 1811 addressed the General Assembly of the Presbyterian Church on the subject.

As the mood and will for improving the nation's life increased, temperance came to be widely seen as an avenue of American progress, sometimes as an intrinsic good. William Miller, one of the popular millenialist preachers of the day, urged temperance in anticipation of the parousia: "For your soul's sake drink not another draught, lest [Jesus] come and find you drunken." More practical reformers, though not beyond alluding to God's wrath, recited "this worldly" rationales for temperance instead of cataclysm. Parson Weems, for example, gave a recipe to avoid drunkenness with injunctions against dueling, borrowing excessively, and the like. "Never marry but for love," went one of the moralisms. "Hatred is repellent; and the husband saunters to the tavern." In the words of Alice Felt Tyler, historian of American reform, "temperance and not abstinence, self-control and not self-denial, was the objective" of most of the early leaders in the movement. According to her account, only the Methodists and the Society of Friends offered concerted urging against the use of hard liquor during the first decade of the nineteenth century.

By 1816, the Methodist General Conference, however, passed a resolution "that no stationed or local preacher shall retail spirituous or malt liquors without forfeiting his ministerial character among us." Such a rule, and there were many more to come, cut into the economics of the frontier church especially. But even on the coast, pastors frequently received some distilled spirits as a portion of their salary, just as farmers and tradespeople dealt often in this convenient medium of exchange.

In 1813, a Massachsetts Society for the Suppression of Intemperance was organized among the Presbyterians and Congregationals in that state. Other scattered groups formed to "suppress intemperance" elsewhere; but not until 1826, rather late in comparison with other formations of benevolent enterprises, was the American Society for the Promotion of Temperance organized. They decided to work for their goal by seeking mass signatures of pledges promising total abstinence. Important figures signed at gatherings with flourishes of a gold pen. Temperance leaders asserted that in 1835 they had received signatures from more than 3000 American ministers. Local, state, and "woman's auxiliary" units sprang up throughout the country seeking like methods for change, and over a million Americans belonged to temperance societies by 1834. "Moral suasion" they thought would accomplish their ends, and even in Congress they moved to have endorsements from Congress members individually. Soon it became apparent that the selling and consuming of liquor continued unabated. At least one bar satirically offered a new drink, "The Moral Suasion."

The American Temperance Society, by 1833 strongest of the national associations, called for stronger measures in response to the problem. In a Convention of that year, they passed a resolution condemning the sale of liquor as "morally wrong." A collection of representatives formed the more tightly knitted American Temperance Union to seek legislation against the "rum trade," to promote abstinence, and to disseminate its point of view. Most of this increased activity came from the northern states, because Southerners found many of the same people advocating temperance and anti-slavery—Garrison and Gerrit Smith among them. As they became defensive of their "peculiar institution," they withdrew from the national movement to remain only locally interested in the effects of temperance. Some Northerners too rebelled at the "ultraism" of this reform. Bishop of Vermont, Episcopal John H. Hopkins, published his attack on the movement in 1836. Temperance was fine, but should not be mistaken for a Christian imperative. There were other, more biblical, measures of piety according to his work, *The Primitive Church*.

At the same time as the societies grew and the opposition to ultraism increased, a third force sprang up of "Washingtonians," men who embraced the gospel of teetotal temperance as reformed alcoholics. Formed in Chase's Tavern, Baltimore, April 2, 1840, the Washingtonians exacted a comprehensive pledge from adherents, employed religious terminology—"salvation," "testimony," and the like—and crusaded mightily for societal reform. They formed under their banner parades and fairs that featured "the Cold Water Army," regiments organized by the Reverend Thomas Hunt about the same time as the Washingtonians themselves. They also sponsored publications, the most popular of which was the inimitable "Ten Nights in a Bar Room and What I Saw There," by fortune-seeking Timothy Shay Arthur. The

Washingtonians, though essentially white male workers who repented of their profligacy, sponsored women's auxiliaries, and at least one chapter was open to black membership. Leaders among them were two evangelists—John Hawkins and John Gough—both tradesmen and eloquent speakers. Gradually their movement lost its solitary luster and joined with the more staid societies as they worked for reform laws.

Success was not too slow in arriving. Between 1841 and 1852 no new licenses were awarded for rumhouses in Boston, for example. Local options began to draw voters to exclude sale of spirits, and finally in 1846 Maine passed a comprehensive statewide prohibition act. A thorough law, known widely as the model for state acts, went into effect in that state in 1851. Vermont passed a similar bill in 1852, Rhode Island the same year. Michigan, Connecticut, Indiana, and others followed suit.

Many reformers interested in temperance had ambiguous feelings regarding the Maine Law. Theodore Parker said "it makes the whole state an asylum for the drunkard." He approved of it in part, but he recognized it "an invasion of private right."

> I believe it will be found on examination that, other things being equal, men who use stimulants moderately live longer, and have a sounder old age than teetotalers. But now I think that nine tenths of the alcoholic stimulus that is used is abused. The evil is so monstrous, so patent, so universal, that it becomes the duty of the state to take care of its citizens; the whole of its parts.

There remained ways around the prohibition laws, for enterprising persons who could purchase goods from other states. There also existed a loophole for the medicinal use of liquor. But consumption did go down demonstrably in the states and territories with laws.

As the Civil War encroached on American life, prohibition took a back seat temporarily to other matters. But most of the laws remained in force, and the impetus that created the laws continued a viable one in American life. Yet to come would be the investment of women in the W.C.T.U., Emma Willard and Carrie Nation, and the Anti-Saloon League. For the present, temperance and prohibition remained a male dominated movement, with the women forming attendant structures to the new groups (the "Sons of Temperance", for example). Women were already moving in yet another reform, however, seeking rights of their own.

Women's Rights

Few women were able to publish their thoughts about sexual equality before the nineteenth century. There are, to be certain, poignant words from Abigail to John Adams that satirically threaten a revolution by women. And more thorough expression can be found in the articles by "Constantia" in the *Massachusetts Magazine* (1790). In those pieces, Judith Sargent Stevens Murray recited some of the discrepancies between American treatment of women and men. "And if we are allowed an equality of acquirements," she promised, "let serious studies equally employ our minds, and we will bid our souls arise to equal strength."

It was not until the 1800's, however, that forceful and widely-heard statements of the situation could be voiced. Women then began to share their hopes for autonomy, opportunity, and at least proximate justice. More than that—they began in small numbers to work for their goals. Angelina Grimké, for instance, spoke out when she felt slighted personally just as she spoke out in favor of freedom for America's black population. In 1838, she wrote to her friend Theodore Dwight Weld describing a lyceum meeting on women's rights. "There our lords and masters undertook to discuss our rights," she complained. She, and a coterie of sisters, would not long remain silent when the men debated. Grimké likened her situation to that of a slave "gagged" in the company of slaveholders conversing about emancipation.

The remark was historically inspired on the part of Grimké, for she and most sisters in the suffragist movement came to discern the issue of women's rights through involvement in anti-slavery. Angelina Grimké (1805-1879) joined her sister Sarah in public lecturing and other means of agitation in behalf of women's rights. Both sisters had moved from Charleston, South Carolina, to Boston and had left their slaveowning family to become Quakers. They gained public forums as "agents" of the American Anti-Slavery Society, but opposition arose to their speaking in front of men as well as women. At least one church body formally protested the public presence of the Grimké sisters, denigrating their contributions to the movement for anti-slavery. The Congregationalists of Massachusetts in 1837 bemoaned the "fall into shame and dishonor" of women reformers who assumed "the place and tone" of men. For her part, Angelina Grimké persisted in her efforts and, with Sarah, presented on the floor of the Legislature of Massachusetts a petition for abolition of slavery signed by 20,000 citizens. It was the first address by a woman to a legislature in the U.S.

Along with the Grimké sisters, Lucretia Mott (1793-1880) presented a similar point of view. She, as the Grimkés, came by pious conviction to the conclusion that she owed American blacks her full efforts. Founding the Philadelphia Anti-Slavery Society with her husband James, she remained as its president and moving force for forty years. As a Quaker minister, Lucretia Mott was also experienced in leading worship, and she readily put her expertise to work for the cause of feminism. She carefully distinguished the sources of oppression of women—social, political, religious. "It is not Christianity, but priestcraft, that has subjected woman," she insisted.

But trouble erupted for the women's rights issue when in 1840 Abby Kelley, another abolitionist conscious of her duty to "speak up" was elected to the business committee of the American Anti-Slavery Society led by William Lloyd Garrison. Garrison himself saw the need of women representing themselves on the various committees, not just contributing money through auxiliaries. But almost half the men in the society withdrew to form a rival American and Foreign Anti-Slavery Society. There women would be prohibited from active leadership. It confused the issue, according to Lewis Tappan and other men of the schismatic group, to have freedom for slaves mixed with suffrage.

Garrisonians sent Lucretia Mott and Elizabeth Cady Stanton to London that fall to attend the World Anti-Slavery Convention. Again the men responded in hostile fashion to the prospect of sharing the convention floor with women. Mott and Stanton lost in their attempts to gain seating as delegates. Rather the men graciously consented to "allow" the women space in the gallery (to hear but not be seen, behind a curtain). There the two women conceived of a plan to assemble a convention of their own, composed of persons interested in and sympathetic to the rights of women.

In 1848, the first convention in behalf of women's rights was called by Stanton, Mott, and other women. The intrepid black abolitionist Frederick Douglass was there, along with two-score other men in the 300 persons seeking proximate equality for women. The call for the convention, based on the text of the Declaration of Independence, declared: "We hold these truths to be self-evident: that all men and women are created equal: that they are endowed by their Creator with certain inalienable rights...." There followed a list of injustices tyranically imposed on women by men, just as the Declaration had listed those of the King. The greatest disagreement arose in the convention, held at Seneca Falls, New York, when they barely passed a resolution to press for voting rights. Subsequent meetings at local, state, and national levels of the suffragists brought publicity to the movement (and opposition, too, mostly ridicule but some violence). More important, the women, and men in agreement with their goals, began re-thinking the stereotypes foisted on females in American society.

After the events of Seneca Falls, women challenged head-on the institutions and authorities of the day. Lucretia Mott, for example, argued in 1854 that "the Bible has been ill-used" venerating man over woman. She commented on the special problems of the church at Corinth, to which Paul wrote his admonitions concerning "woman's place."

> It is not so Apostolic to make the wife subject to the husband as many have supposed. It has been done by law and public opinion since that time. There has been a great deal said about sending missionaries over to the East to convert women who are immolating themselves on the funeral pile of their husbands. I know this may be a very good work, but I would ask you to look at it. How many women are there now immolated upon the shrine of superstition and priestcraft, in our very midst, in the assumption that man only has the right to the pulpit, and that if woman enters it she disobeys God.... Believe it not my sisters.

Rather than submit to such oppression, women should re-interpret the tradition in "truth," showing that Christianity sought to break the barriers between people and free the prisoners. Subsequently, Stanton would produce a *Woman's Bible* expounding on these ideas.

After Seneca Falls also, a new generation of women moved to lead the suffragist cause. Susan B. Anthony (1820-1906), a Quaker, a fine organizer, and a colleague of Stanton, had not attended the first convention. She heard of it from her parents who had been there. She worked first with Amelia Bloomer on a paper, and through her met Stanton. Together the two formed a Woman's New York State Temperance Society, another example of the reforms working hand in hand. She saw to completion the first suffrage successes in New York State too, when property laws were modified in 1860 at her insistence.

Lucy Stone, another feminist leader and the first female graduate of Oberlin where coeducation had been an experiment, was a Unitarian. She came to feminism even before she worked for abolition, one of the few women in ante-bellum America to do so. She lectured in winsome fashion throughout the northeast. When she married Henry Blackwell, a "fellow" worker in reform, she kept her name (much to the chagrin of many proper Americans). With Anthony and Stanton she formed the Women's Loyal National League during the Civil War in order to seek passage of the laws finally accomplished in the Thirteenth Amendment.

Later splits would emerge as the movement developed, but early solidarity characterized the women's rights advocates. And at least temporarily, the feminists remained staunchly loyal to religious ideas and ideals, seeking to move within the communions to bring enfranchisement to women in them. At the same time, they sought to put their faith to work on the larger society, seeing the churches as an avenue of resolution even if they also formed part of the problem.

Anti-Slavery Reform

Anti-slavery reform indeed lay at the very heart of the benevolent enterprise. Many if not most of the colonial and Revolutionary proponents of emancipation drew upon their theologies to fashion a response to the "peculiar institution" of chattel slavery. From the wide spectrum of anti-slavery forces came a majority of the temperance, women's rights, universal education and pacifist leaders. Scores of reformers seeking uniform Sabbath observance, child labor laws, and other specific causes had found their voice in anti-slavery. Elizabeth Cady Stanton, already cited, met almost all the nationally known reformers when as a young girl she saw them at the home of Gerrit Smith, the long-time advocate of anti-slavery in Peterboro, New York. Charles Loring Brace, later acclaimed for his pioneering efforts in the rehabilitation of children and delinquents, acknowledged anti-slavery as one source of his interest in the "underdog" of society. Sojourner Truth, who moved into agitation for free land for freed blacks, began her career as an abolitionist. Some, like

Horace Mann, came from concerns for other reforms—care for the insane and education for all—to embrace political anti-slavery. To be sure, the reforms did feed each other, but anti-slavery appears still the focus of the whole spectrum of reform.

If anti-slavery was the spawning ground for reform, then abolition was for thirty years at least the core of anti-slavery-ism. Before 1831, signal date for the beginning of immediate abolitionism as an articulated American alternative, anti-slavery had been a more moderate movement. Much, if not most, feeling for emancipation had been generated in the slave states themselves. The American Colonization Society, for example, seems to have gathered more strength in the South than in the North with its sincere but ineffective cries for gradual (sometimes compensated) manumission. Anti-slavery Quakers in the south expressed abhorrence of the system. And in 1798, Henry Clay, Father David Rice, and others worked to outlaw slavery in Kentucky's new state constitution. They almost succeeded.

Even when during the 1820's the South began to silence opposing voices in their midst, abolitionist expressions were only scattered among the general feelings for anti-slaveryism. George Bourne, a Virginia Presbyterian minister, had already been sent packing in 1817 on trumped-up charges of heresy after he published some thoughts about immediate freedom for blacks. John Holt Rice, a prominent Virginia clergyman in the same communion, ceased to speak out on the subject during the 1820's. But still in 1827, of 130 anti-slavery societies in the U.S., 106 were in slave states. The great majority of these groups, North and South, favored moderate reform. A major ingredient in this program of moderate change was the expatriation of free blacks, a threat to black lives and careers that did not go unchallenged. Blacks began efforts to insure that their own anti-slaveryism would be heard, and that their right to remain in the U.S. would be honored.

The year 1831 remains important in the chronicle of reform for at least two reasons—William Lloyd Garrison began in January of that year to publish his *Liberator*, and Nat Turner in the same August led his ill-fated uprising which served to scare Southerners forever with the paranoia of armed rebellion by blacks. Garrison, son of an evangelical Baptist mother (his father deserted the family), was apprenticed as a sober, religious young man to Isaac Knipp, a printer in Newburyport. Later he moved to Boston, then to Baltimore as a partner of Benjamin Lundy, a Quaker printer, in the publication of the *Genius of Universal Emancipation*. Only after exploring many meager possibilities did Garrison initiate the *Liberator*. Blacks evidently bought most of the copies, although Arthur Tappan subscribed heavily to help underwrite Garrison's effort. So too did Ellis Gray Loring and Samuel Sewell. According to Louis Filler, historian of anti-slaveryism, James Forten of Philadelphia paid for 27 subscriptions and other black people were instrumental in helping the paper survive. Filler contends, however, that Garrison's reputation was made by intransigent southern proslavery forces, more than by any northern solidarity for his position. Early northern violence toward Garrison did not hurt the cause he represented, either. A close colleague in the movement, Wendell Phillips, recounted that the sight of Garrison being hauled bodily through the streets of Boston by rowdies convinced him to join in the efforts of such a person.

Whatever his sources of power, Garrison turned antislavery reform and abolitionism into synonyms. He labored continually from religious presuppositions—that God was on his side, that freedom was the divine intention for all, and that people who saw the light would turn to it.

For his part, Nat Turner was also a religious person. He led more than fifty slaves from Southampton County, Virginia, on the basis of a divine call to action. Apocalyptic and prophetic strains of biblical influence radiated from Turner's "Confession," garnered after his capture. A number of whites were killed in the process of Turner's revolt, and the Virginia militia retaliated by murdering almost every one of the insurgents. That a slave uprising could occur, however, so frightened the Southerners and their supporters in the north that they cooperated in rigidifying the codes regulating black behavior in the slave states. Moreover, due to ignorance probably, (or was it their paranoia?) Southerners linked the uprising with the new *Liberator*, and they began to surmise an abolitionist plot to overthrow the slave system.

The "golden era" of abolitionism saw the development of hundreds of anti-slavery societies, some comprised of evangelical Christians, others primarily of liberal religionists, but with most groups encompassing both. Historians have long argued without resolving the issue whether Garrisonian or "Western" abolitionism was the more potent movement. The latter, headed by James G. Birney, concentrated on political ways of ending slavery. First through the creation of a Liberty Party, and then with alliances elsewhere, the political abolitionists concentrated on social structures being changed. In 1840, and again in 1844, Birney ran for President. From an Alabama slaveowning family, Birney grew to abominate slavery as a morally contemptible system. He struggled through first the American Colonization Society then the American Anti-Slavery Society to end it. Forced gradually northward, Birney moved in 1833 to Kentucky, subsequently to Cincinnati, and finally to New York. A fall in 1845 left Birney partially paralysed and cut short his public career, but he continued to symbolize political abolitionism as a real alternative for ending slavery.

Assisting Birney in political abolitionism was Theodore Dwight Weld (1803-1895), a convert of Charles G. Finney, and a veteran of his "holy band" of revivalists. Preparing for ministry, Weld enrolled in Lane Seminary and agitated for abolition among the students, faculty, and Cincinnati townspeople as well. Forced to leave the school by Lane's trustees, Weld convinced many students to go with him to Oberlin.

There, and subsequently throughout the North, Weld operated as organizer for the American Anti-Slavery Society. He
oversaw the formation of teams of speakers, and he married
one of his group, Angelina Grimké in 1838. He also managed
time to write a number of tracts, including the formidable
American Slavery As It Is, an exposé upon which Harriet
Beecher Stowe based her momentous *Uncle Tom's Cabin*.
Weld kept his political sense, and served as an advisor to anti-
slavery Representatives and Senators during the stormy years
before the cause became so patently attractive to politicians.
New York, Ohio, as well as other "Western" units among the
abolitionist societies identified with Birney and Weld.

Garrison, on the contrary, willingly adopted "disunionism"
as an anti-slavery device. He led whole segments of the movement, particularly in New England states, into thinking of the
issue as more a "personally moral" one than as a political one.
Although the contrast can be overdrawn, agents of Garrison-
ianism sought personal "conversion" and attitudinal change,
dissociation from slavers, as a way of bringing the reform to
fruition.

In the middle, Quaker groups long devoted to abolition of
slavery sought to work for its accomplishment through boy-
cotts of sugar, cotton, and rice—all slave-made goods. Lucretia Mott and others led in this middle way of anti-slaveryism.

Gradually the several prongs of anti-slaveryism together
collected results. That mainstream communions began to split
over the matter was one evidence that it took on increasing
importance in religious life in the country. In addition, a
whole generation of former slaves now abolitionists and freedom fighters for sisters and brothers occupied public podia
and published accounts of their experiences. Harriet Tubman,
Sojourner Truth, Frederick Douglass, and a score more blacks
began to tell their stories, and on a national scale.

Anti-slavery politicians began to crop up in positions of
power, too. William H. Seward, first as Governor of New
York and then as that state's Senator, Salmon P. Chase and

Benjamin Wade from Ohio, Gerrit Smith and Joshua Giddings, not to mention the redoubtable Charles Sumner— voiced uncompromisingly anti-slaveryism. Wade was a religious skeptic, but most of the rest came to their opinions from religious traditions they imbibed and sought to live.

As the course of the reform progressed, attempted compromise pleased few indeed. Especially the Missouri Compromise of 1850, enforcing the Fugitive Slave Law while providing for a "free D.C." and other non-slave territories, served only to heighten feeling on both sides. Northern abolitionists were incensed at the prospect of having free blacks returned, sometimes to a slaver who had no "legal" right to take them. Many cities experienced riots when federal marshals sought to enforce the law. The Southerners likewise perceived a threat to the institution by now considered necessary to their survival. It made of Daniel Webster a "traitor" in the eyes of many Northerners, and ruined his political career. In short, with the failure of compromise and the advent of "Black Republicanism," the irrepressible conflict was at hand.

7

Toward a Christian War

In his second inaugural address, Abraham Lincoln lined out for brothers and sisters the irony of America's "Second Revolution." The period under consideration had begun with a quest to "Christianize" the newly formed nation. It ended with a holocaust in which two sectional parties sought in the final stages of the conflict to damage each other as much as possible. "Both read the same Bible, pray to the same God; and each invokes His aid against the other," Lincoln lamented.

Methodists and Baptists split in anticipation of the division in the nation, and so too did the Presbyterians, if their theological reasoning hid beliefs about slavery under it. Episcopal and Old School Presbyterian churches split when the war commenced. Reform movements gravitated about the anti-slavery core and its pro-slavery backlash. Indeed Lincoln summarized that "core" also with his remark that "One-eighth of the whole population were colored slaves. . . . a peculiar and powerful interest . . . somehow the cause of the war" and everybody knew it.

Still three factors must be discussed in order to complete a cogent picture of religious ingredients in American life during these decades. Seemingly diverse in nature, they found meeting points in the conflict and in consequent American life. White racism, black religious organizations, and the theology of Lincoln himself become the subject matter for this final study.

White racism began and continued as an American religious dilemma. It permeated not only the ethics of Christians
with power in the country, but constituted a major force in
the church life of America as well. Many whites brought their
opinions of black inferiority with them from Europe, while
others learned to discriminate on the basis of color once here.
There were exceptions, to be sure, people even in ante-bellum
American leadership who espoused human equality that did
not mean merely "equal opportunity." The great preponder-
ance of whites, however, agreed on their superiority to black
people in political, social, and even religious sensibilities.

At the same time, a black religious life grew into organization and influence during these decades. Slave religion was
part, but not all, of it. Free blacks gained a sense of institutional belonging through the church, and the black churches
already by the time of the Civil War set their directions in
large measure retained today.

And the political theologian Abraham Lincoln gave rise to
an American civil religion which has come to be accepted in
American popular piety. He not only believed, but gave
eloquent voice to, the dogma of "divine democracy." At a
personal level his religious sensitivities remained sound and
at times almost approached being revelations in themselves.
But as translated in American life, the ideas of God's judg-
ment and wrath have lost something of the theological edge
they had in Lincoln's own articulations. He also provided
personally the inculcation of these ideas and ideals in his
presidency. Thus his religion becomes extremely pertinent for
American religion.

The White Problem

"These critters an't like white folks, you know," Haley, the
slavetrader remarked to Mr. Shelby in *Uncle Tom's Cabin*.
The Southerner was generalizing on his understanding of
Eliza's feelings about Harry, her son. Haley's statement was
fictional, but Stowe's insight a real one into the perceptions

of most white Americans of the day. The "white problem," which has been usually termed "the black problem," arose from that misconception.

White racism ran deep in America, and all three of the theologians considered in chapter five, shared it to some degree. Hodge, for example, spoke seldom in print about the "inferior class" of blacks in America. But he did so at least once in the review of William Ellery Channing's *Slavery*, written for the *Biblical Repertory* of 1836. There Hodge declared that the institution was both biblical and humane, despite frequent lapses in southern treatment of slaves. The duty of Southerners, as Hodge saw it, was to "improve" the slaves rather than to liberate them. "If the fact that the master and slave belong to different races, precludes the possibility of their living together on equal terms," he maintained; "the inference is, not that the one has the right to oppress the other, but that they should separate." But Hodge noted further, "Whether this should be done by dividing the land between them ... or by removal of the inferior class on just and wise conditions, it is not for us to say." Hodge concluded the notation with a word of praise for the colonization movement, "one of the noblest enterprises of modern benevolence."

Bushnell's racism was the more apparent, for he produced a book on the subject of "evil," *The Moral Uses of Dark Things*. In that work, not published until 1868, he gave a whole chapter, "Of Distinctions of Color," to the question of black people living in America. There he reiterated his previous consideration of the black as an "outsider" in the U.S., "as if their color was the stamp of night on their history, both past and future." Bushnell sought abolition of slavery, but he also sought white dominance over black America. He fully anticipated no free black presence in a future U.S. "My expectation is that the African race, in this country, would soon begin to dwindle towards extinction ... if emancipated," he had earlier declared.

Even Theodore Parker, much revered among Boston's free black people and a first-rank abolitionist, entertained thoughts of an "entirely Anglo-Saxon" Western hemisphere. Whether in satire or in straight prose, Parker stated on more than one occasion that "the Anglo-Saxon disdains to mingle his proud blood in wedlock with the 'inferior races of men.'" There remains for Parker the possibility that he envisioned a new race emerging in the U.S. composed of black, white, and red people in harmony. However some of his assertions, as the one above, certainly left hearers an open possibility of judging him a white racist.

That theologians did not rise above the cultural racism of their day may be regrettable, but it is not surprising. Their sentiments were shared by such "heroes" as Thomas Jefferson and Abraham Lincoln. Jefferson, for example, thought that black people needed less sleep, accommodated themselves better to strenuous labor, and experienced more "transient" grief than whites. Considering only American blacks, he further claimed:

> Comparing them by their faculties of memory, reason, and imagination, it appears to me, that in memory they are equal to the whites; in reason much inferior, as I think one could scarcely be found capable of tracing and comprehending the investigations of Euclid; and that in imagination they are dull, tasteless, and anomalous.

Scientists undergirded popular opinion among whites with appropriate research and "findings." They focused investigations on the "Chain of Being," in which all "creation" could be perceived as a hierarchy. Anatomical structure especially was employed to "prove" that blacks existed in a state lower than whites and more beastial. Louis Agassiz of Harvard developed an enthnological theory of white supremacy that remained exceedingly popular through ante-bellum years.

Thus the impetus for slavery received backing from many Northerners and almost all Southerners during the decades immediately preceeding the war. What alternatives were there for black presence in America if slavery ceased? The Southerners argued that slavery was biblical, and they contended that southern culture was Christian. Noah's "curse" they interpreted racially, and they linked that hermeneutic with the existence of slavery in New Testament times. By this interpretation of the Genesis account, Ham was made black as a curse because he sinned against Noah's God. Thus Ham's descendants were black, the link with their progenitor. Some Southerners even believed that Ham sinned in attempting amalgamation of the races, and that he received divine punishment for that unpardonable sin. They did not bother to follow closely the narrative, in which no mention of blackness occurs. Instead they read the command of Leviticus (25) that permitted the buying and selling of slaves. To compound their argument, Jesus nowhere condemned the practice; and Paul even returned an escaped slave to his master (Philemon).

To be morally upright, argued southern moralist James Henley Thornwell, a Presbyterian leader, the slaveowner is obliged to treat his property according to the "Golden Rule." "The rule then simply requires, in the case of slavery, that we should treat our slaves as we should feel that we had a right to be treated if we were slaves ourselves." Thornwell and other southern apologists admitted that as it existed the institution was imperfect. But southern culture remained Christian and sought to progress in its institutions. Slavery was a way of raising the status of women, and southern white women represented a "new hope" for the world in their virtue and civilization. In addition, the church permitted whites and blacks alike the opportunity to improve their lives, and to achieve salvation according to God's plan for the world. William Harper of South Carolina, the son of a Methodist minister, went so far as to term slavery "the principle means" of improving humanity. Seen as a progressive institution, slavery was to be defended by all, and not just the slaveowners of the south.

White racism also provided the impetus for much of the anti-slavery sentiment in the North and West. Most midwestern abolitionism came from opposition to the expansion of the institution, for instance. Many towns specifically and by law actually excluded free blacks from owning residences in them. In other communities, tacit agreements among merchants and property owners kept blacks from holding jobs or buying and renting homes in them. In the 1850s Michigan, Wisconsin, and Iowa, in revising state constitutions, excluded free blacks from voting on the basis of public referenda. Exclusionists even sought state laws prohibiting black people from settling in them. By the same token, moves to support black emigration from America ("Ohio in Africa" was just one) received considerable support.

Further west, white prejudice was almost as rampant. White Californians solidly endorsed the exclusion of slavery, and in the compromise of 1850 the state received recognition. But their aboliton of the slavery formerly practiced by some there was accompanied by another prohibition—blacks could not vote or serve in the state militia. A provision to exclude blacks entirely from the state failed to carry in the convention after a spirited debate concerning its effects. Evidently the framers of the constitution worried that its provisions would jeopardize federal approval of the document and impede statehood. Oregonians too voted restrictions on blacks alongside abolition. Free blacks were allowed to leave Oregon in peace, but those staying would risk periodic floggings.

This kind of white racism prevailed even during the Civil War. "Draft riots" focused on black people, and many northern blacks perished in northern cities because whites vented their frustrations and class feelings on them as cultural "scapegoats." In all this the churches frequently sought to bring harmony to the society, but just as frequently racist sermons and suggestions by church members of possible actions led to increased oppression in ideology and activity of black America.

Southern opinions during the war did not change direction, but merely gained in intensity. Their commitment to human hierarchy drove the Confederates to scorn the ideas of equality, democracy, and freedom voiced in former American documents. "If the mischievous abolitionists had only followed the Bible instead of the godless Declaration, they would have been bound to acknowledge that human bondage was divinely ordained," declared Thomas Smyth of Charleston's Second Presbyterian Church. Later in the war, hard put to continue the fighting, Southerners even considered freeing the slaves. They did not do so, however, because they remained convinced the blacks were inferior. In the expression of historian H. Shelton Smith, they kept living their racism "to the bitter end."

The Black Church

The one institution among American black people giving them impetus for liberation was their church. To be sure, other, external forces and institutions were at work in behalf of black freedom—international relations; northern reform movements for education and justice, especially anti-slavery; some commercial systems; and portions of the mainstream, white church all conspired to end slavery. But among American blacks only the church proved available for the great majority as the locus of learning human solidarity, exodus from oppression, human potential, divine interest, and other basic ingredients of freedom.

That some slaves were not permitted even to participate in church activities at all remains a testimony both to the cruelty of the system and to the power of the Judeo-Christian tradition as a potential for liberation. Among some white communions in the South discussions and debates were recorded concerning the wisdom of "colored evangelism" (occasional theologians even wondering aloud whether black people possessed souls)! Underlying these considerations was the ever-present threat in the U.S. of a slave revolt inspired by the religion believed by whites and blacks alike.

Long before the revolt of Nat Turner, another Virginian named Gabriel planned a rebellion based on the identification of himself with Samson and his fellow slaves as the Israelites. News leaked out and the Gabriel plot of 1800 was aborted by arrests and convictions of more than forty slaves. According to Gayraud Wilmore, historian of the black church in America, other similar revolts were planned by slaves who read about Moses, Judges, and Christians in the Bible.

Another case in point was that of Denmark Vesey in South Carolina, charged in 1822 with 130 other blacks of fomenting an insurrection against the system. Vesey himself was a free person, belonging to the local A.M.E. congregation, and evidently was advised in his efforts by the Reverend Morris Brown. Protracted meetings at the church were probably the occasion for plotting the revolt, for when a white Charlestonian wrote of them, he decried their "noisy, frantic" spirit and supposed the congregation engaged in "many evils." Furthermore, when 67 persons were either hanged or banished after the pseudo-trials, all belonged to that church, and the building itself was destroyed. The church was suppressed.

On the other hand, whites who believed their own racist interpretation of the Ham story, the epistle to Philemon, and the Pauline injunctions were generally willing, if not eager, to spread the gospel among the blacks—especially among the slave population. They considered it a means of following the missionary imperative to preach and baptize. At the same time, they considered Christianity a religion that undergirded institutional slavery and taught "obedience to masters." All the while whites saw that proper supervision of black churches did not repeat Gabriel, Vesey, and Turner experiences.

White churches frequently had black galleries, where slaves and sometimes free black people could sit for worship. Prince Johnson, a former slave, remembered that his owners in Clarksdale, Mississippi, did not allow slaves to learn reading or writing. All the slaves were "taught to be Christians," however, and attended church with their owners. He said the "Mistress" forbade the wearing of charms and the practice of voodoo. "Everything on that place was blue stocking Presbyterian," he said. Likewise he remembered that slaves would gather informally on their own when possible to pray and sing. Thus an informal, black church existed for them alongside the official, white one.

With the separation of the A.M.E. and the A.M.E. Zion communions from the Methodist Episcopal Church, numerous black congregations grew up affiliated with no white church at all. Likewise black Baptist churches arose on their own, even before the American Revolution. Their number increased significantly as white Baptists in the north lost an earlier zeal for emancipation. At the same time southern whites were moving into positions of influence in the various associations. Of particular note was a black congregation, the African Baptist Church in Savannah, led by former slave George Liele. Another slave minister freed to preach in the same city was Andrew Bryan. Companion congregations of independent black people sprang up in every major center throughout the east and south.—Philadelphia, New York, Boston, Washington, Cincinnati, Detroit, Chicago, Jacksonville, Florida, Lexington, Kentucky, and other places.

South Carolina, according to the pioneering study of black church history by Carter G. Woodson, offered a special situation in that blacks there were prohibited by whites from belonging to separate congregations. Thus in that state all congregations formally were dominated by whites, in leadership if not in numbers.

A generation of black clergy and lay leaders grew to fill the needs of the church. Charles Bennett Ray, a Congregational minister in New York, Henry Highland Garnett, a Presbyterian pastor first in Washington and then in New York, and Leonard A. Grimes, a Baptist minister in Boston, were but three of the several score of educated clergy and organizers in mid-century America's black church. It was Grimes who typically fought the removal of Anthony Burns from Boston under the Fugitive Slave Law. When those efforts failed, he raised the $1325 required to buy freedom for the man. Similar evidence of independence on the parts of Ray, Garnett, and a host of other leaders argues for the essential integrity of the black church as a separate institution in antebellum America.

The backbone of the slave church was also the preacher, although little can be learned of the people who exercised that function in the rural south. "My father was the preacher and an educated man," recalled Daniel Dowdy, a former slave. "You know the sermon they gave him to preach?— 'Servant, Obey Your Master'. Our favorite baptizing hymn was On Jordan's Stormy Bank I Stand. My favorite song is Nobody Knows the Trouble I've Seen." The songs and the prayers of the slave church were subtle words for freedom.

Cooperation of black churchpeople lay at the heart of the subterranean escape plans of various slaves. All the ministers mentioned above, together with hundreds of other church folk North and South, assisted through channels now known as the "Underground Railroad." It may well be, as Larry Gara has argued, the Underground Railroad was not thoroughly organized as its legends now proclaim it to have been. Surely Levi Coffin, John Rankin, and other white Christians helped escaped slaves along in their quest of freedom in Canada. But as Gara points out, white people have been over-emphasized in the freedom movement. Black abolitionists and slave colleagues have been comparatively ignored.

The black church was, according to Wilmore, "the cutting edge of the freedom movement among both slaves and freemen." Another historian of the church, Benjamin Quarles, states flatly that the black church alone could "speak out on such an issue as slavery without fear of losing members or offending someone in the South." Many scholars have credited the Underground Railroad in particular, and the anti-slavery movement in general, with "causing" the war. Certainly black churches greeted the war with greater enthusiasm than their white counterparts. Some white ministers declared that once the war had begun, emancipation should be proclaimed immediately for black slaves. George Cheever of the Church of the Puritans, and Henry Ward Beecher of Plymouth Church were two of the most vociferous. Unitarian Henry Ward Bellows was another, asserting that "what best serves God and humanity best serves basket and store." Not all white sentiments were crassly commercial as were Bellows', but they paled alongside the efforts of blacks.

William Waring of Toledo declared that blacks would be given a new existence by the war. Leonard Grimes was out organizing Boston's black soldiery on the day after the war began (although it would be years before they could serve). Charles Lenox Remond, John S. Rock, Lewis Hayden, and other black abolitionists maintained their status during the war, as lecturers for black and white. They in turn labelled the war as a "holy cause." Blacks recruited, when finally permitted by Lincoln to do so, and the regiments marched to war. According to Woodson, they sang not only "authorized" patriotic songs, but their own "freedom songs" as well for marching tunes:

Oh, Freedom! Freedom over me!
Before I'd be a slave,
I'd be buried in my grave
And go home to my Lord and be free!

Black churchpeople, just as many whites, looked to Abraham Lincoln as the paragon of religious idealism in the cause of freedom. His occasional participation in the racism of his day did not deter them from revering the President as a religious, as well as a political, leader.

Lincoln's Cosmopolitan Christianity

Quakers, Disciples of Christ, Catholics, Presbyterians, Spiritualists, Methodists, Unitarians, and Baptists have all claimed that Abraham Lincoln was an adherent of their respective communions. He was married to Mary Todd by the Reverend Charles Dresser, an Episcopal priest. Many of his evangelical opponents accused him of being an "infidel." But Lincoln apparently succeeded in being all of these, and none of them, at the same time. His presidency and his leading of the Union focused Americans on the vitality of their religious traditions, as well as upon the precarious nature of their status as God's "chosen people." Thus his own theology and religious life, enigmatic as they seem to have been, become germane to the story of the times.

Lincoln's parents were members of the Little Mount Separate Baptist Church, an evangelical congregation that believed strongly in the anti-slavery cause in southern Indiana. After his mother Nancy Hanks Lincoln died, Abraham's father Thomas remarried and led in the formation of the Pigeon Creek Baptist Church, probably "hard-shell" in doctrine. Lincoln himself evidently did not join the church; but his later knowledge of and affection for Scripture, as well as his articulated "doctrine of necessity" would remain consonant with the predestinarian and "Bible-believing" Baptists from his early childhood.

According to biographers, Lincoln questioned the sectarian Christianity of the Methodists and the Presbyterians he saw in power when he moved to Illinois. He read Thomas Paine's *Age of Reason* which supplemented his doubts about the validity of Protestant orthodoxies. Soon after also "reading" law, he began service in the Illinois legislature.

When he stayed in Springfield with Joshua Speed, Lincoln discussed with his friend not just his romances but a growing awareness of "reverence for the laws." Public addresses—to the Young Men's Lyceum (1838) and to the local Washingtonian society (1842)—accented the centrality of justice and American obligations to make democracy succeed as a social experiment. In private correspondence with Speed, who returned to Kentucky in 1841, Lincoln declared his primitive faith in God's providence. And when he married Mary in 1842, Lincoln attended the Episcopal Church with his wife.

Lincoln returned to private practice in 1849. When his son Edward Lincoln died in infancy and the Reverend James Smith conducted the funeral, Mrs. Lincoln joined that Presbyterian Church and Abraham attended there with her without joining. Lincoln did maintain respect for Smith throughout life, however, and read the pastor's apologetic work, *The Christian Defense*, one of the few works in theology he ever confessed having perused. William J. Wolf, studying Lincoln's religion, found striking parallels between the theology of Smith and Lincoln's later religious expressions. But his law partner William Herndon was also feeding Lincoln works by Theodore Parker at the same time. Many of Lincoln's ideas, not to mention some of his very expressions, are published in works by Parker available during the years of Lincoln's public life. Parker, for example, had declared that democracy is government "of the people, by the people, for the people" some years before Lincoln "coined" the phrase. In addition, sporadic accounts by free thinkers and others show Lincoln following Parker's theology in his reading.

Returning to public life in opposition to Stephen A. Douglas, Lincoln moved to embrace more consciously the problem of slavery in his theology as in his politics. He also embraced the newly forming Republican Party. Having lost in initial skirmishes, Lincoln ran against the powerful Douglas head-on in the Senate race of 1858. "I believe this government cannot endure permanently half slave and half free," he declared. Douglas answered Lincoln's "house-divided" speech with allusions to the implications of emancipation. "This Government is founded on the white basis..." Douglas maintained. "Preserve the purity of our Government; no amalgamation, political or otherwise, with inferior races."

Lincoln responded to Douglas with other possibilities. If exceptions were made to the rights granted people in the

Declaration of Independence on the basis of·color, "Where will it stop?" "If one man says it does not mean a Negro, why not another say it does not mean some other man?" What began as syncopated speeches turned into a series of face-to-face debates. Douglas, of course, won the race; but Lincoln gained the ear and the allegiance of increasing numbers of Republicans. When in convention politics he gained the nomination for President, his popularity and the complicated matters of Democratic schisms managed to conspire for his election. Elected, his words and actions led the nation during those crucial years of the "Second Revolution."

The theology Lincoln articulated as President mixed civil religion, evangelical concern, and the ethics of higher law. According to Wolf, Lincoln seldom resorted to any distinctly Christian categories such as references to Jesus, "the savior," or "the Holy Spirit." Rather he confessed faith in the God of history, Almighty God, the Lord of the Universe. Prayer, by Lincoln's standards, did not change God's direction of events but rather sought human harmony with divine intent. The Bible, which by all accounts Lincoln continued to read devotionally during his years at the White House, offered "the best gift God has given to man" for ethics and faith. Often even Lincoln's humor revolved around sayings of the prophets, or Jesus, and of other biblical personages. As for church, he attended Sunday worship and sometimes midweek services at New York Avenue Presbyterian Church where Old-Schooler Phineas D. Gurney was the pastor.

In public life, specific religious commitments Lincoln declared sometimes resonated with popular piety, but often his assertions ran counter to such faith. He explained his actions in proclaiming emancipation for slaves in rebellious states by reference in a cabinet meeting to a kind of bargain with God: "I made a solemn vow before God, that if General Lee was driven back from Pennsylvania, I would crown the result by the declaration of freedom to the slaves." Whether Lincoln reacted to a "tit-for-tat" prayer, out of character with his other religious sentiments and statements, or whether he perceived divine confirmation of a course already chosen, cannot be gleaned from research thusfar. More profound statements, his oratory of the address at Gettysburg and his second inaugural, show Lincoln a scrupulous theologian and a religious genius. How shall the human cost of war be reconciled with God's loving care? "That we here highly resolve...that this nation, under God, shall have a new birth of freedom." Dying and destruction he linked with birth and creation.

Again, how can the South be religious and keep slavery? "It may seem strange that any men should dare to ask a just God's assistance in wringing their bread from the sweat of other men's faces; but let us judge not, that we be not judged." Whether Americans perceive it or not, God continues to operate in justice and mercy.

The noted British theologian of the time, F.D. Maurice, declared that Lincoln returned American religion from its democracy of the Declaration of Independence to its more original theocratic state. "In so far as it recognized the divine vengeance for the wrongs of the colored race," Maurice said, "it implied a Christ as Head of the human race." More probably Lincoln moved Americans into new horizons in their civil religion. He seems to have revered the Declaration of Independence and the democracy represented in it as almost canonical in authority. Moreover, his primary intention remained throughout the war to "preserve the Union." He sought to inculcate compassion, wisdom, and forebearance into the very office of the Presidency. And he mixed evangelical Christianity (minus its sometimes parochial view) with the theology of natural law already inherent in the basic American documents.

Granted, as he expressed to the New Jersey Senate, Lincoln did view Americans as "God's almost chosen people." But the subtleties soon departed as Americans took up the religious outlines Lincoln concocted. And "sacred democracy" was passed to all of us, an American heritage, along with a passion for "law and order," which can become demonic if not qualified by reverence for human life and for justice.

8

Epilogue

At mid-century, historian Robert Baird summarized the fervor of the period in his conclusion to *Religion in America*, written first in 1842 to explain to Europeans the promise of the new nation's faith. "Our religious liberty, unbounded and precious as it is, is not the cause of the success which has attended the Gospel in America. It is only the *occasion*, ... not the *means*, by which the Church of Christ has made so great advances in the United States." Baird looked to Sunday Schools, Bible classes, reform societies, Home Mission societies, "Maternal associations," and "the *preaching of the word*" as major instrumentalities in bringing about a Christian nation. But, with characteristic American modesty, he had to admit that God was the primary "means" of the nation's achieving its greatness. "Surely God has led His people to expect a great outpouring of His Spirit in the 'latter days'." Baird likewise admitted there remained much to be done for the evangelical cause in the United States. Especially did the evil of slavery demand eradication. However he predicted inevitable progress, church growth, and gradual sanctification of the nation's corporate life.

By the time of the Civil War's end, many Americans North and South had come to recognize that the nation would not become, in fact, a Christian one. Jewish people, and persons of other religious faiths, shared at least peripherally in the

132

pluralism. Among the mainstream Christians, moral fervor bent upon itself to diffuse both energies and ideals. Themes of the era would endure—with increasing explicitness of "manifest destiny" and "frontier" especially in years to come. However the benevolent enterprise, the utopian preoccupation, the transcendetalism all passed at least temporarily from America's center-stage. What endured were the strengthened institutions—the various communions of Baptists, Methodists, Reformed, Catholic, Episcopal, Lutheran believers. The vibrant new denominations and sects, issues in dissent and schism from the mainstream, achieved uneasy civil and ecclesiastical detentes with their "spiritual parents." Benevolent organizations remained also, the American Bible Society among the most notable of the interdenominational brand. Other efforts had been absorbed largely into denominational structures—mission, publication, and Sunday School efforts particularly. Civil Rights, suffragist, and other reform groups would come in time to build on foundations established during America's new nationhood, but only after a hiatus of sorts. Most of all, pluralism was here to stay.

In the words of William Warren Sweet, historian of the frontier church, "this formative period" of American religion set the tone for generations to follow. It was a time of people in motion, "vast streams of them, each and all moving away from the old home, the old community, the old school, the old church, and the restraints and influences which all of these things imply." Americans managed to provide a measure of continuity together with innovation, as Sweet saw it.

There were leaders—Lincoln above them all, but also the Bushnells and Parkers, Hodges and Motts, Emersons and Douglasses, and scores more. These people lived noteworthy lives, provided models for post-war generations. But increasingly less formidable personalities led in various places and movements, a democratization had at least begun in American patterns of leadership. Church and cultural leaders would surely rise in years to come, but their ideas and achievements would contribute to the pluralism rather than to recapture any sense of homogeneity.

And the story would continue unabated of American religion, its vitality and idiosyncrasies, its institutions and persons, its movements and contributions to American life in general.

DATE DUE

OCT 23 1980			
NOV 13 1980			